2018

The Sociological Return

METHODOLOGY & SOCIAL MEDIA

DR ROB WATSON

ISBN-13: 978-1725611566

ISBN-10: 1725611562

Author: Rob Watson

https://decentered.co.uk

Leicester, United Kingdom

August 2018

Dr Rob Watson

Contents

1   Social Collaboration

Social media is defined with a heightened emphasis on collaboration and shared techniques of production that are not expected of other, more traditional forms of media. This distinction is often characterised as a set of working and conceptual practices that are grounded in a real-world environment, in which *individual* and *collaborative* knowledge is often blurred and indeterminate. Our understanding of the importance of the everyday practices and experiences of the participants who use social media might be explained, on the one hand, as a form of social knowledge that is exchanged within a *'societas'* (that is a group of people who share their corresponding life experiences together); or alternatively, as a set of social arrangements that takes the form of a *'universitas'*, (in which there is a mutual self-interest between a group of people who want to achieve a particular goal or outcome). To put this in some context, and as Richard Rorty explains:

> "Epistemology views the participants [of a community] as united in what Oakeshott calls an *universitas* – a group united by mutual interests in achieving a common end. Hermeneutics views them as united in what he calls a *societas* – persons whose path through life have fallen together, united by civility rather than by a common goal, much less by common ground" (Rorty, 2009 p.318).

The question that arises, therefore, is:

- *To what extent are we able to make sense of the collaborative knowledge practices that take place in social media groups?*

Is it possible to establish the basis on which participants in these communities of *interest*, *identity* and *practice* are able to understand their *role*, their *identity* and their *accomplishments?* Furthermore, to what extent do these communities of interest and correspondence, reflexively understand themselves as either a *universitas* or as a *societas*, or a blending of both? In what way can we develop a pragmatic picture of the *casual correspondence* and the *contingent relationships* that 'fall together' within fieldsites of community and collaborative media, with the assumption that this picture will open-up space for further discussion about the basis on which *collaborative purpose* is arrived at in these communities.

1.1   Collaborative Knowledge Practices

In attempting to locate this presumed sense of common purpose, either as a society based on shared goals, perhaps articulated in radical dreams of critical emancipation or utilitarian efficiency; or a society of correspondence, in which people just rub-along together, it is necessary for any investigation to focus on some practical tasks that might prove useful in wider discussions. These tasks include "predicting the behaviour of inhabitants" of the unfamiliar cultures of social media groups; learning to talk with different agents within overlapping social media groups, despite the "incommensurability of [their] language" (Rorty, 2009 p.350); and, the development of practical models that participants, advocates and users of social media can reflect on to improve the effectiveness and competence of their ethical and practical operations.

1.2 Language Mapping

According to Richard Rorty, by mapping out the *commensurable* and the *incommensurable* terms within our languages and social routines, we should be able to identify and distinguish what is *new* from what is *old*, what has *changed* from what *remains the same*, and what is *useful* from what is *redundant*. This is a pragmatic approach in which the adage, *that we can strip away anything that doesn't make a difference*, applies at all times. And while this might not seem to be particularly 'deep' or 'critical' set of aims or inferences, when compared with other more classically or critically oriented forms of social analysis, the degree to which this analysis may provide insightful as part of a wider discussion of emerging cultures of social and collaborative media should prove to be insightful. The aim of pragmatic social thinking, according to Rorty, is to provide a space through which "commonsensical practical imperatives" can be validated against "the standard current theory about subjects" (Rorty, 2009 p.385). But as McCarthy and Wright affirm, "pragmatists theorising is [more of] a practical, consequential activity geared toward change, not representation" (McCarthy & Wright, 2004 p.20).

The task at hand here, therefore, is to link and validate the commonsensical practical imperatives of people who are working in social media groups and networks, with the standard ideas and concepts that are associated with the analysis of social media, and then come up with some practical suggestions that might help in pursuing change on the ground – both in the social media groups in practice, and in the formulation of the prevailing ideas and concepts associated with the study of social media.

2 Sociological Objectives: What Can a Sociological Outlook Achieve?

The value of the ethnographic model lies in its ability to reflexively identify information from within complex, dynamic and transient social activities (Schensul, Schensul, & LeCompte, 1999). While quantitative research methodologies are able to distinguish and characterise large-scale social issues, through a process of calculation and statistical analysis, what is not readily identified using these techniques is the process by which social actors find meaning in their activities. As a qualitative form of research, ethnography aims to narrate how social groups negotiate and allocate legitimacy for the meanings that they build-up in practical usage.

Ethnography is therefore concerned with the process of accumulated meaning as derived through social practice and experience. Ethnographic study puts a particular emphasis on how these meanings accord to contingent relationships, between different actors in temporary social groups, and how these relationships change and shift as social norms change and shift. This means that ethnographic study is able to ask questions about social relationships, such as how perceptions of on-going social and symbolic status are founded and regulated through, for example, power-related discourses of domination or subordination? Or, what happens when new technologies are introduced to a social environment that changes the productive and cognitive capabilities of different participants of emergent communities? In short, "ethnography tries to understand practices, relationships, and cultures from the inside" (McCarthy & Wright, 2004 p.34), with the provision that qualitative research, as Uwe Flick notes, does not seek to study "artificial situations in the laboratory, but the practices and interactions of everyday life" (Flick, 2009 p.15).

2.1 Anthropological and Sociological Traditions

At its most basic level ethnography emerges from a series of anthropological and sociological investigative traditions. It can be thought of as a disciplined form of social enquiry that seeks-out an accountable and practical approach to the study of culture. As Boellstorff *et al* suggest:

> "Cultures, as shared systems of meaning and practice, shape our hopes and beliefs; our ideas about family, identity, and society; our deepest assumptions about being a person in this world" (Boellstorff, Nardi, Pearce, & Taylor, 2012, p. 1).

It is therefore incumbent on ethnographic investigators to "attempt to develop an understanding of how a culture works" (Bell, 2005, p. 17), and to describe and explain the many factors and historical movements that shape our cultural and social interactions. Put simply, "ethnography is a method for understanding culture" (Hine, 2005, p. 8). An understanding that is founded in a shared affinity with the people being studied, and a sense of responsibility toward the use that those studies might be applied. As Boellstorff *et al* specify, in ethnographic investigation:

> "The goal is to grasp everyday perspectives by participating in daily life, rather than to subject people to experimental stimuli or decontextualized interviews. Ethnographers often speak of their work as 'holistic'. Rather than slicing up social life according to variables chosen for their contribution to variance in a statistically drawn sample, ethnographers attend to how cultural domains constitute and influence each other" (Boellstorff et al., 2012, p. 3).

The objective of this discussion, then, is to map out and identify some of the issues that are associated with, and that are representative of, the process of ethnographic study and the techniques that are broadly used to support this form of enquiry. The aim is to counter the claim that Glaser (perhaps ironically) makes, that "methodology is something that everyone tells others to follow and that everyone does not want to be told by others to follow" (Glaser, 1998, p. 4). Instead, what will be offered here is an attempt to account for the process of enquiry in principle, and as a result, offer some assessment of the individual actions that are required in ethnographic study in practice. Emerging from this will be a template that fits these techniques together as a recognised and shared set of principles and practices that are capable of underpinning repeat processes of social enquiry.

3 Structure or Structures of Feeling?

To relate this discussion to its wider context, it is worth recalling what C. Wright Mills described as the *Sociological Imagination*, and the extent to which practitioners of ethnographic investigation are bound to seek an affinity with both the immediate personal scenes in which they find themselves (our milieux), and the wider historical and social forces that shape those personal interactions, identities and biographies. For Mills "the sociological imagination enables its possessor to understand the larger historical scene in terms of its meaning for the inner life and the external career of a variety of individuals" (Mills, 1959, p. 5). It is a false option (if we are to follow Mills guidance), to attempt to understand the actions of individuals purely from an instrumental point of view, as if their social exchanges are merely transactional or the product of determining forces, as in some economic or psychological traditions.

Likewise, it is equally false to assume that people's social actions may only be defined through complex social processes and historically determined movements, as in some moral, structuralist or political science traditions. As Mills describes:

> "Perhaps the most fruitful distinction with which the sociological imagination works is between 'the personal troubles of milieu' and 'the public issues of social structure.' This distinction is an essential tool of the sociological imagination and a feature of all classic work in social science" (Mills, 1959, p. 8).

And it is with this tradition in mind that an ethnographic methodology for the study of social media will be outlined, described and evaluated here. This methodology aims to show and illustrate the personal milieu of practitioners working in real social situations in which social media is enacted and practiced. These situations, on the one hand, might be said to be *structured through the economic and historical contexts of an interactive and engaged culture*; while on the other hand, they can be said to be *an interplay between the social structure and the agent that shapes and defines the perceived or imagined options of actors who are in play*. The predominant school of thought underpinning this approach, therefore, is *pragmatic, interpretativist* and *social-constructivist* in its philosophy and outlook, and draws substantially on the work of Herbert Blumer and Robert Prus and the tradition of symbolic interaction (Blumer, 1953, 1966, 1969, 1990; Blumer & Shibutani, 1973; Prus, 1996, 1997, 1999).

3.1   Understanding Social Life

Prus points out that the qualitative approach is convenient to our understanding of social life, and the forces that shape the human condition. Prus warns, however, that the way that we talk about these forces cannot be given-over entirely to positivist explanations and narratives, because, as Prus argues, any reification of the positivist tradition involves taking for granted and losing sight of the "ways in which human behaviour is accomplished in practice, by living, acting, interacting minded beings within a community context" (Prus, 1996, p. 245). For Prus, the ethnographic tradition is a practical form of investigation that aids us as we enquire about, and seek to understand, the human condition, and the practical situations under which that condition finds its "shape, expression, and very essence." As Prus elaborates:

> "In contrast to the postmodernist, who tend to reduce human experience to textual reality, and the positivists, who tend to reduce human lived experience to structuralist reality, it is argued [here] that human existence is predicated on people coming to terms with the day-to-day situations in which they find themselves" (Prus, 1996, p. 245).

Ethnography, therefore, is the study of human values, and the expectations that we have about how we live, behave and associate in our practical social lives. These are values that might often be determined through the routine enactment of social norms and established patterns of behaviour, but more often, as Mills suggests, they are values that are subject to patterns of learning. As Mills points out:

> "That these shared values are learned rather than inherited does not make them any less important in human motivation. On the contrary, they become part of the personality itself. As such, they bind a society together, for what is socially expected becomes individually needed" (Mills, 1959, p. 31).

When people share the same values, it is generally expected that they have a tendency to behave in accordance with the patterns that have been established in a social group or community, and usually we treat such conformity as a very good thing – even when it seems to go against our immediate individual desires. On regular occasions, however, social change is manifested when the general expectations and social norms that we have grown familiar with are shifted and challenged – as a result of either technological, cultural or historical social pressures. It is therefore incumbent on the ethnographer to be able to deal flexibly with these emergent social situations, that they may not be familiar with or fully cognisant of. The ethnographic researcher, therefore, has to maintain a high level of flexibility in their approach if they are to make sense of the changes and norms that take place around them. Being "sensitive to the contexts we study" (Boellstorff et al., 2012, p. 3), is therefore an abiding principle that will be applied here.

4   Hypothesising or Describing?

At this point it is useful to note some key features of the ethnographic investigative tradition, and the challenge of producing shared knowledge on the basis of social interpretation and understanding. As Boellstorff *et al* remark:

> "Ethnographic research is fundamentally distinct from experimentations; the goal is not to determine how controlled variables account for difference, but to trace and interpret the complex currents of everyday life that comprise our collective lived experience as human beings" (Boellstorff et al., 2012, p. 3).

Therefore, the concepts and the methods of inquiry that are identified in this overview should be a reminder that not all scientific approaches are quantitative and experimental, and that instead, ethnographic studies are able to address issues that are *indeterminate*, *ad-hoc* and *allusive*. In other words, they can be conceived as the partial and biased accounts of individuals who maintain a personal perspective, an intimate biography, and many conflicting and contradictory lived experiences. These biased accounts and stories, it has to be noted above all, are the very things that give the ethnographic approach its authority, as they offer an underpinning for the values and accomplishments that we seek to describe and share in our investigations.

The expectation is that the stories and the words of the people we are talking to are the most useful way for us to reflect on our shared cultural experiences from multiple perspectives. Because it is through these shared stories that we are able to pass-on ideas, histories and a sense of identity, and also to draw inferences, lessons and morals that might be learnt by newcomers to the discussions. The value of these accounts to the individuals means, therefore, that participants in any field study must be respected on equal terms as co-researchers. Subjects of any ethnographic study have to be valued for their individual voice and for their unique point of view, something often forgotten in large-scale, mechanical and institutionalised research practices.

4.1   Interpretation and Description

Ethnographic research, it should be noted, is interpretive and descriptive, and eschews positivistic testing and hypothesising in order to make sense of the complex social processes that are at play in a given subculture or social milieu. As Boellstorff *et al* point out, in the ethnographic tradition:

> "We rely on field observation, not experimentation; we develop explanations rather than predictions; and we use qualitative methods (though not exclusively). But these moves do not mean that ethnography is not empirical or rigorous" (Boellstorff et al., 2012, p. 31).

Seeking to test hypothesis implies, according to Boellstorff *et al*, that social scientists would be working "within the horizon of the known" (Boellstorff et al., 2012, p. 32), because they are working within a framework of theoretical data analysis that is deductive and empirical. The choice of the theoretical framework that social scientists use can reflect and shape the kinds of outcomes that they are able to predict from their studies, and as Boellstorff *et al* go on to point out, "even purely quantitative studies require human intervention and interpretation"(Boellstorff et al., 2012, p. 37).

The ethnographic tradition, however, takes a different approach, as it is based on inductive and/or adductive reasoning. Somewhat frustratingly for many researchers, the lack of an early-stage hypothesis in an ethnographic study might imply a perceived lack of structure, (accompanied therefore by a large amount of anxiety), but as Glaser points out, it is important that ethnographic researchers "do not argue in the beginning," but instead, "do the research and see what emerges as a dissertation defence" (Glaser, 1998, p. 18). According to John Creswell, for the large part of the ethnographic study theory should be absent, with a greater emphasis instead given to description and to the elaboration of expositionary "guides" (Creswell, 1998, p. 87). The question arises, however, about how data can be corroborated or applied if the ethnographic researcher has little sense of "its meaning or significance in advance" (Boellstorff et al., 2012, p. 83)? As Creswell explains:

> "In a qualitative study, one does not begin with a theory to test or verify. Instead, consistent with the inductive model of thinking, a theory may emerge during the data collection and analysis phase of the research or be used relatively late in the research process as a basis for comparison with other theories" (Creswell, 1994, p. 95).

4.2   Inductive Processes

This inductive process is one in which the observations that are made and recorded are "built up in order to make more general statements about a phenomenon" (Kozinets, 2010, p. 119). Inductive analysis is a way to manoeuvre the recorded data that has been collected over the whole of the study, rather than seeking to make a wider claim of validity based on inferences determined from 'cues' and 'samples' of representative operational responses. This generalisation remains grounded in the phenomenological nature of the material and is validated on the basis of the appropriateness of the selection process and the "relevance of findings and the reflexivity of proceedings" (Flick, 2009, p. 15).

Issues of validity are central to the successful reception of an ethnographic study, but the forms of validity that are expected are not deducted or extrapolated from experimental findings, instead the researcher surveys the field and develops an intimate account of the social interactions and exchanges that take place there. As Creswell states: "a qualitative researcher works inductively, such as when he or she develops categories from informants rather than specifying them in advance of the research" (Creswell, 1998, p. 77). These categories 'emerge' from the informants themselves, and cannot be predicted in advance by the researcher. As Creswell also notes: "this emergence provides rich 'context-bound' information leading to patterns or theories that help to explain a phenomenon" (Creswell, 1994, p. 7).

It is the researcher's role, therefore, to look for patterns within these emerging social phenomenon, and to suggest categories and themes that may link them together (or with other wider preoccupations). This is an emergent process that cannot be built into the design specifications of the study. Instead theories may emerge late in the research process and serve as the "basis for comparison with other theories" (Creswell, 1994, p. 95). Ethnography, as such, does not start with a hypothesis to test or verify, so the methodologies that are deployed have to evolve and change in response to the data that is collected in operation.

At the early stages of the study the ethnographic researcher "may advance 'tentative' definitions [only,] because the precise definitions as used in a study will emerge from the conversations with informants in a study" (Creswell, 1994, p. 107). So rather than establishing a theoretical model and hypothesising, then experimenting on controlled sample objects, the ethnographic researcher has to manage simultaneous activities running at the same time – collecting information through fieldwork, reflecting on the information and assigning categories to it, then developing a wider narrative of observations that form the shared textual summary of the investigation. As Creswell explains:

> "Data analysis requires that the researcher be comfortable with developing categories and making comparisons and contrasts. It also requires that the researcher be open to possibilities and see contrary or alternative explanations for the findings" (Creswell, 1994, p. 153).

The outcome of an ethnographic study, therefore, is highly descriptive, narrative based and contextual. It does not seek to offer *proof* or to make claims through which positivistic change can be brought about as a consequence of the investigation. Instead it seeks to describe, comment, draw inference and inductively connect what was once lived-practice. Practice that has been transmuted through the recollections of agents, and which might never have been connected with wider themes and ideas had the researcher not spent time observing, listening and reflecting on the situation.

5 Positivist vs Interpretative Traditions

While "there are many various qualitative research traditions, such as phenomenology, social constructionism, social constructivism, grounded theory, ethnomethodology, symbolic interactionism and naturalistic inquiry" (Struwig & Stread, 2001), it is not likely that any research project will focus exclusively on any one single or bounded research methodology, but may instead pull from a range of different and blended approaches in order to suit the circumstances of the environment, the participants that are being studied, and the available resources at hand for the researcher. Mike Crang and Ian Crook discuss how the linear nature of ethnographic research planning can be a hindrance when starting a field-based study. What they describe as the "read-*then-do-then*-write model" of research design (Crang & Cook, 2007 p.3) can often present a problem for the ethnographic researcher when they later engage in field-based data collection.

If an ethnographic research project is designed, according to Crang and Cook, on the basis of first outlining *in principle* a sustained literature review and theoretical modelling process, then when the researcher enters the field they may not be prepared for what they encounter. The researcher may not be able to recognise or conceptualise the phenomenon encountered, and may therefore be unable to record important elements of this field activity, as they do not fit the researchers prior established methodological framework.

5.1 Research Processes

Crang and Cook recommend that ethnographic research should be developed, instead, *in practice* and on a "piece-by-piece" basis (Crang & Cook, 2007 p.3). This does not imply that research design and planning should be chaotic and extemporary, but rather, that research design should be regarded as a process that develops on the basis of continuous feedback, interpretation and reflection. Robert Prus gives voice to the frictions that have been recognised when the two traditions of social science are reviewed and compared - the *interpretive* and the *positivistic*. As Prus notes:

> "The central problem [...] is that mainstream social science does not respect the nature of human group life. In not adequately acknowledging the interpretive, interactive essences of people's lived experiences, these approaches fail to achieve intimate familiarity with their subject matter. Thus, despite claims of a scientific enterprise, conventional (positivist) social science contributes little understanding of the ways in which human group life is accomplished" (Prus, 1996, p. 70).

Similarly, and according to Crang and Crook, researchers should be able to develop their research question and hypothesis at the same time as developing their case study and their methodological rational. Crang and Cook see no problem with approaching the design, the collection of data, and the reporting of analysis in a non-linear series of interconnected and parallel techniques that are "grounded" and "process-oriented" (Crang & Cook, 2007 p.3). The expertise required of the researcher in these circumstances is reliant on their ability to keep an open mind to the possibilities presented by the situations that their tentative research leads them toward. A researcher should be able to keep control of any parallel processes by project managing and coordinating these parallel activities in a way that is strategic, goal oriented and feedback focussed.

5.2   Ranges of Factors

It is for this reason that many research projects of this kind are scoped on the basis of a *deferred* definitive practical methodological statement. So, and as a consequence, studies of this type instead addressed a range of corresponding organisational, methodological and theoretical factors as the project progresses. In effect, the organisational focus of this type of methodology shifts from the abstract and the theoretical, to the practical and the phenomenological. Operational questions about project management, resource allocation and continuous feedback and review of performance, take precedence as indicators that illustrate how a project might progress. This is a pragmatic approach that talks about *appreciation* over and above *experimentation*. As Robert Prus points out:

> "Human existence is predicted on people coming to terms with the day-to-day situations in which they find themselves. What is required is a pragmatic appreciation of the human life-world as it is accomplished by people acting and interacting with others in community settings, on a day-to-day, moment to moment basis" (Prus, 1996, p. 27).

5.3   Countering Instrumentalism

Prus is weary of debates and arguments associated with the structuralist traditions of social science enquiry, regarding them as inadequate and insensitive to the communities and people who are being studied. However, Prus is equally weary of the organisational and management style of analysis (the instrumental analysis of statistics and systems) that has emerged in more recent times. Prus calls for the study of human life as a form of *accomplishment* that is interactionist and interpretative, and which is underpinned by a conceptual base and methodological capability that prioritises the "way of life of a group of people" (Prus, 1996, p. 103). As Prus notes

> "It has become increasingly apparent that structuralist approaches are inadequate for comprehending (and studying) the processes by which human interchange takes place, but the alternatives (humanistic, Marxist, postmodernist, narrative) with which people in the organisations/management field have been working lack both a conceptual base and a methodological capacity for examining the human production of organisational life" (Prus, 1999, p. 28).

The alternative to the positivistic approach, according to Prus, is to recognise the potential participants in any study to be an *interpretative community*. In an interpretative community the common bonds of association are mediated through utterances, acts, accomplishments, actions, texts and through the writing and producing of symbols of social communication. As Gale Miler asserts:

> "Such communities consist of shared orientations to social reality and interpretive practices that like-minded readers and writers bring to their reading and writing of texts. To say that interpretive community members are like-minded is not to say, however, that they are of one mind. Indeed, interpretative communities may involve diverse conflicts of interest and interpretation, but these conflicts are negotiated within contexts made up of community members' shared assumptions, concerns and interpretative practices"(Gale Miller in Miller & Dingwall, 1997, p. 8).

5.4   Shifting Toward the Intersubjective

The implications of this conceptual shift toward an *intersubjective* experience will be explored in more detail later, however, it is sufficient to say at this point that this is a sugnificant area of debate and discussion that is well represented in the schools and disciplines of the social sciences. In some quarters the idea of researchers prioritising an *intimate familiarity* with their subjects is problematic, while in others, it is celebrated and prized. Robert Kozinets summarises the relevance of the intersubjective and interpretative approaches:

> "Interpretivism is a school of thought devoted to the goal of understanding the complex world of lived experience from the point of view of those who live it, a phenomenological perspective. The criteria underlying interpretive anthropology favour grounded meanings, richly detailed or thick description, and use the metaphor of reading and interpreting a complicated text for the reading of a given culture"(Kozinets, 2010, p. 160).

6   Qualitative vs Quantitative Techniques

It is worth noting for a moment, then, the distinction and difference between the qualitative and the quantitative model of enquiry, if only to further draw-out the underpinning justifications for the ethnographic style of investigation. It is now generally accepted that each researcher will bring with them a worldview or a sense of schooling to any particular study. Those worldviews will favour assumptions and biases that are part of the tradition of enquiry that the researcher has learnt and been schooled in – the paradigm of experience and established truths. These "methodological assumptions", however, are themselves heavily imbued with social practices and social ambiguities, in the same way that the phenomenon being studied may be found to be imbued with "ontological, epistemological, axiological, rhetorical, and methodological assumptions" (Creswell, 1994, p. 8). It is a key facet of the qualitative approach, therefore, that researchers deal with this biases in two important ways: firstly through methodical reflection; and secondly, because the qualitative mode of investigation is inherently "exploratory" (Creswell, 1994, p. 21).

The researcher is generally interested in a social topic or aspect of community life because little has been written about it. The best way to find out more about social phenomena is to speak directly to informants who have experience of them and to observe their actions, from which the researcher can then build a narrative or story. In contrast with the established methodological traditions of the quantitative approach, which seeks to check the internal validity of social phenomenon with an objective external validity, the qualitative approach recognises that there are no generalisable terms that can be surmised from social investigation, or an objective position from which social phenomenon may be judged. Instead, and according to John Creswell, the ethnographic researcher "may employ terms such as credibility, transferability, dependability, and confirmability, as well as naturalistic generalisations." As Creswell notes, "words such as understanding, discover, and meaning form the glossary of emerging qualitative terms and are important rhetorical markers in writing purpose statements and research questions" (Creswell, 1998, p. 77).

6.1   Non-Linear and Practice-Based Research

Furthermore, qualitative research often comes against criticism that it has little to ground it with a sense of internal coherence. This claim is made because of the competing traditions, which see studies based around so-called standards of *quality* and *linearity*. Ethnographic researchers often find a great deal of resistance and inertia when they propose that a research study can take place using non-linear, practice-based and reflexive approaches. When the techniques of quantitative research are compared to the heavily institutionalised and technically invested quantitative techniques, it is natural that they will seem so much more uncertain - based as quantitative techniques are on repeatability, sequential linearity and empirical measurement. As Uwe Flick explains, in quantitative forms of enquiry, the "process of research can be neatly arranged in a linear sequence of conceptual, methodological, and empirical steps.

Each step can be taken and treated one after the other and separately" (Flick, 2009, p. 90). The steps taken in the quantitative process are mutually interdependent and offer reassurance that in following the agreed steps some intended outcome will be arrived at. It is entirely possible, however, that the qualitative models of research may produce no such certain or easily understood results of any kind at all. Which obviously induces a further sense of vertigo and anxiety for the research team and their supporting institution, who have to financially plan, predict and meet research assessment targets. For those interested in pursuing a qualitative research study, then, the bottom line is that they have to be content simply that they are demonstrating *curiosity* about a topic or phenomenon that is otherwise little known, otherwise emergent, and may even have been socially discredited or marginalised. If little is known about the subject, then there are few known or validated variables that can be referred to as markers or signs of its existence and importance. They are intangible.

So, the ethnographic researcher is unlikely to be able to draw on established theories to guide their studies, "because those available are inadequate, incomplete, or simply missing" (Creswell, 1994, p. 10). The variables are largely unknown, and the researcher wants to focus on the context that may shape the understanding of the phenomenon being studied, and so in many qualitative studies a theory base does not guide the study. Uwe Flick explains how in the:

> "Traditional version of quantitative social science starts from building a model: before entering the field to be studied, and while still sitting at their desks, the researchers construct a model of the assumed conditions and relations. The researchers' starting point is the theoretical knowledge taken

from the literature or earlier empirical findings. From this, hypotheses are derived, which are operationalised and tested against empirical conditions. The concrete or empirical 'objects' of research, like a certain field or real persons, have the status of the exemplary against which assumed general relations (in the form of hypotheses) are tested. The aim is that you want to guarantee that your study is representative in its data and findings (e.g. because random samples of the persons that are studies are drawn). A further aim is the breakdown of complex relations into distinct variables, which allows for researchers to isolate and test their efforts. Theories and methods are prior to the object of research. Theories are tested and perhaps falsified on the way. If they are enlarged, it is through additional hypotheses, which are again tested empirically and so on" (Flick, 2009, p. 90).

6.2   Instrumentalist Research

In this sense quantitative research is focussed on concrete subjects that have delineated and bounded presence in a location or at a time. Measuring actions or surveying responses and collecting statistical information over a series of activities and functions, which suggests that all facets of human life can be studied if they can be apportioned to a measurement heuristic and subsequently instrumentalised for data analysis. This approximation of the physical sciences suggests, as Robert Prus argues, that a "human being can be studied in manners analogous to other objects"(Prus, 1996, p. 206). This point is well illustrated by Judith Bell, who advises researchers who are new to the process of collecting social data:

> "Survey can provide answers to the questions What? Where? When? And How?, but it is not so easy to find out Why? Causal relationships can rarely, if ever, be proved by survey method. The main emphasis is on fact-finding, and if a survey is well structured and piloted, it can be a relatively cheap and quick way of obtaining information" (Bell, 2005, p. 14).

The quantitative thrust, then, is on objectivity and causation, with data being conceived as interchangeable from lived experience to statistical comparison. While these metrics may be useful and do provide many sources of insight that have been richly mined by the social sciences, they are not value-free *in themselves*, and so in many circumstances can offer little in the way of new insight, comprehension or understanding. Seeking to challenge the quantitative bias of social science practice, Robert Prus has suggested that:

> "The emphasis on operationalisation (instrumentalism), quantitative analysis, and (qualified) structural causation have generally remained dominant in mainstream social science, as have hopes of developing a coherent, cumulative social science that reflects a synthesis of data gathered on these manners" (Prus, 1996, p. 207).

6.3   Objectivity and Causation

According to Prus the "quantitative thrust with its concurrent emphasis on objectivity and causation has become the methodological nexus of mainstream social science" (Prus, 1996, p. 208). This positivist/structuralist approach, places emphasis on patterns and routines of data collection behaviour, and places restrictions on the cognitive diversity that researchers are able deploy when they approach topics and communities. Firstly, there is a narrowing of the types of subjects that can be studied and the places or situations that they can be studied from. If it is not 'observable' then it is of no use in the quantitative approach. Secondly, there is heavy emphasis placed on the way that a social phenomenon is thought to emerge from existing structures or antecedent conditions. Thirdly, by standardising the methodology and the techniques of observation there is a further restriction of what can be recorded, i.e. that which can be translated, usually, into mathematical or process-oriented models. Next, is the issue of hypothesis testing and the way that results and data must be reproduced in order to be verified. And finally, once this data is scaffolded into an empirical framework it then has to be generalised along the lines of existing models to be recognised and validated as applicable (Prus, 1996, p. 207).

6.4   Risk Aversion

Thus the quantitative forms of positivistic social sciences are risk-averse, and as John Creswell notes "a researcher who engages in a quantitative study seeks out this paradigm because it offers a low-risk, fixed method of research without ambiguities and possible frustrations" (Creswell, 1994, p. 9). As a result, the researcher would have a truncated period of time to spend on the study. Prus laments the consequence of this because:

> "In attempting to model themselves after the physical scientists, these scholars have not only disattended to the human capabilities of reflectivity, action, and interaction, but they also have been relatively oblivious to the interpretative and interactive nature of all scientific enterprise" (Prus, 1996, p. 209).

It is not within the remit of this paper to challenge or contest the wider viability of the social scientific approach, rather it is simply worth noting that the point made by Prus is that all social scientific approaches can be interpreted and analysed themselves as a "matter of human activity," one that is "fundamentally intersubjective" in its nature (Prus, 1996, p. 214).

7   Reflexive Investigation

According to Gale Miller "whatever the research objectives, qualitative research involves the methodological study of socially organised settings" (Gale Miller in Miller & Dingwall, 1997, p. 3). The implicit difference when contrasted with the quantitative model, however, is that the values and the biases of the investigator are acknowledged and clearly play an active part in the research process. The "investigator admits the value-laden nature of the study and actively reports his or her values and biases as well as the value-laden nature of information gathered from the field" (Creswell, 1998, p. 76). This is what makes qualitative approaches different, because "researchers interact with those they study, whether this interaction assumes the form of living with or observing informants over a prolonged period of time, or actual collaboration" (Creswell, 1994, p. 6). The objectives or qualitative research are to *describe* and *analyse* the processes through which these *forms of living* are constructed, and the sense of reality that people get through their interactions and connections.

How do relationships emerge? How do people connect? How do institutions facilitate those connections? How do these connections form into a *community*, a *culture* and develop into a *society*? What is it that keeps them going, that renews them and brings new people into them? This is a view of intersubjective community life that is "built from the 'bottom up'. They are interactionally constructed realities and patterns of social relationship" (Gale Miller in Miller & Dingwall, 1997, p. 3). And it is this ability to connect across seemingly divergent and distinctive social environments that the qualitative form of research particularly lends itself. The thinking style is inductive; the researcher is concerned with developing narratives that emerge from the observed interactions as they have been designated in categories and themes. Rather than establishing a pre-designed investigative process, the ethnographic researcher follows themes that emerge from the field in a manner that is changeable and variable, and as much as possible without predetermination. As Miller elaborates:

> "Conceptualising qualitative research methods as standpoints involves appreciating the interpretative implications of different qualitative research techniques and analytical frameworks. Qualitative methods are positions taken by qualitative researchers for observing institutional settings. Thus, both the descriptions of social reality that might be constructed by qualitative researchers, and the meanings that they might assign to the descriptions, vary depending on their observational and analytical position. Treating methodological choices as standpoints also directs attention to how some of the most important interpretive possibilities of qualitative studies are established prior to data collection" (Gale Miller in Miller & Dingwall, 1997, p. 6).

7.1 Validating Experiences

So, it is from these *stances* and *standpoints* that qualitative research gains its purpose. Validating experience and emerging thoughts, behaviours and relationships that otherwise "elude quantification" (Boellstorff et al., 2012, p. 38). In the act of observing and recording the ethnographic researcher may well have no idea in advance what is significant about the phenomenon that they are observing. Piece by piece the data that is collected in the form of stories and narratives which may not make much sense on its own, but when they are assembled together, what was once narrow can be seen in the light of similar instances and correspondences. Therefore, it is possible to conceive and elaborate the cultural logics that they reveal, which in turn suggests other areas of future study (Boellstorff et al., 2012, p. 97). As John Creswell notes "Besides dialogue and understanding, a qualitative study may fill a void in existing literature, establish a new line of thinking, or assess an issues with an understudied group or population" (Creswell, 1998, p. 94).

In this way the researcher "builds a complex, holistic picture, analyses words, reports detailed views of informants, and conducts the study in a natural setting" (Creswell, 1998, p. 15). What remains for the researcher to establish are:

- The most appropriate methods and theories.
- A recognition that the analysis will come from multiple perspectives.
- The reflections of the researcher on their role in the process.
- Confirmation that the variety of approaches have worked well in a holistic sense, if not in an individual sense.

The ethnographic researcher, then, selects topics precisely because they are not easy to explain, or because little is written about them. Known variables are limited, there are few theories that explain the witnessed behaviours, and those that do exist need to be developed. Often there is a pressing need to explain the topic in more detail and to present a more thorough overview of the phenomenon. Ethnography is dependent on the central principle of observation in the field, and so researchers spend time interacting with people in their natural settings. Sharing time with individuals and groups in the places that are familiar with and would normally live.

7.2   Pre-Planning Guides

Typically traditional forms of positivist social sciences would establish a detailed plan and literature review in advance of the fieldwork, but as John Creswell notes, "a detailed plan would not suffice given emerging issues that develop in a field of study," because "some issues are problematic for the qualitative researcher – such as how much literature should guide the study, and whether one needs to verify or report on the accuracy of his or her account." According to Creswell "how one addresses these issues shapes the form of the qualitative narrative differently from traditional social and human science research" (Creswell, 1998, p. 18). And so, the format for ethnographic studies vary extensively from more established quantitative and linear forms of research. The ethnographic researcher is working within a process that reflects an interest in *writing* and *discussion* that is more *literary* and *observational* because the researchers' own reflections on their participation in the data collection process are integral to the study.

The role of the researcher as an "active learner" who can "tell the story from the participants' view rather than as an 'expert' who passes judgement on participants" is a priority for this form of study (Creswell, 1998, p. 17). As Creswell elaborates:

> "Writers agree that one undertakes qualitative research in a natural setting where the researcher is an instrument of data collection who gathers word or pictures, analyses them inductively, focuses on the meaning of participants, and describes a process that is expressive and persuasive in language" (Creswell, 1998, p. 14).

Both qualitative and ethnographic investigation are, therefore, forms of social scientific undertaking that represent a "legitimate mode of social and human science exploration without apology or comparisons to quantitative research." As Creswell states, "good models of qualitative inquiry demonstrate the rigor, difficulty, and time-consuming nature of this approach" (Creswell, 1998, p. 9). At the end of the day, and as David Silverman argues:

> "If there is a 'gold standard' for qualitative research, it should only be the standard for any good research, qualitative or quantitative, social or natural science. Namely, have the researchers demonstrated successfully why we should believe them? And does the research problem tackled have theoretical and/or practical significance?" (David Silverman in Miller & Dingwall, 1997, p. 25).

It is possible to summarise the main points at issue in qualitative research as follows:

- "Qualitative researchers are concerned primarily with process, rather than outcomes or products.

- Qualitative researchers are interested in meaning – how people make sense of their lives, experiences, and their structures of the world.

- The qualitative researcher is the primary instrument for data collection and analysis. Data are mediated through the human instrument, rather than through inventories, question-naires, or machines.

- Qualitative research involves fieldwork. The researcher physically goes to the people, setting, site, or institution to observe or record behaviour in its natural setting

- Qualitative research is descriptive in that the researcher is interested in process, meaning, and understanding gained through words and pictures.

- The process of qualitative research is inductive in that the researcher builds abstractions, concepts, hypotheses, and theories from details" (Creswell, 1994, p. 145).

7.3   Flexible Design Approaches

Qualitative study, then, is recognised as a flexible and adaptable form of research that can be applied to many social settings, offering insights into the beliefs and behaviour of social actors that more quantitative method-ologies are unable to achieve. The aim here is to substantiate this approach to data collection in practice, and to ensure that the stories that are drawn from the milieu of social media, with its many active participants, have a narrative coherence and consistency that can be re-applied in different situations and at different times. Ethnographic analysis allows the investigator to observe the actions and the behaviours of participants involved in a specific social situation, rather than relying on reported or inferred approaches, as is considered in other forms of historical recording or journalism. And because theory and hypotheses are *not* established *before* the qualitative research is undertaken, ethnography can make assertions that differ significantly from studies that are reliant on quantitative methods of analysis. That said, it is important to note that the ethno-graphic researcher is regarded as the "primary instrument in data collection rather than some inanimate mechanism" (Creswell, 1994 p.163), and as such, the information that emerges from this qualitative study is likely to be more descriptive, evaluative and reflexive, than the statistical empirical information that is associ-ated with quantitative studies. It will be a priority of this study, therefore, to identify how these differences are articulated, and are manifested through practical application.

8   Empirical Observation

It is worth noting at this point how classical forms of empiricism that have informed the social sciences are challenged by the methodological assumptions associated with ethnographic study. Any form of study that is open-ended in the way that qualitative forms of research are, has problems on two fronts. Firstly, how does the researcher assimilate and manage the potentially large amounts of data that an ethnographic study can generate? And secondly, how does the researcher know when to stop collecting data? What are the saturation points that are arrived at in both of these instances? As Boellstorff *et al* remark:

> "Ethnographic analysis involves a rigorous appraisal of a massive amount of data spanning participant observations, interviews, artefact collection, historical research, and content analysis" (Boellstorff et al., 2012, p. 40).

Therefore, data collection cannot be left to chance or undertaken willy-nilly and without some structuring or organising principles. As Mills reminds us:

> "It is commonly recognised that any systematic attempt to understand involves some kind of alternation between (empirical) intake and (theoretical) assimilation, that concepts and ideas ought to guide factual investigation, and that detailed investigations ought to be used to check up on re-shape ideas" (Mills, 1959, p. 74).

The problem, as Mills goes on to note, is "'how to get down to facts' yet not get overwhelmed by them; how to anchor ideas to facts but not to sink the ideas". As Mills suggests, the problem is "first what to verify and second how to verify it" (Mills, 1959, p. 125). This is the point at which the verification process of recognised methodologies become pertinent. Data collection in an ethnographic study is not done in a way that *only* pleases the researcher, but is instead done with the aim of producing a shared narrative account that can be recognised by the community of scholars and researchers in which the researchers are themselves situated as a community (i.e. in accord with the reflexive impulse). Research communities are like any other intersubjective community of practice, in that they emphasise and debate rules of presentation and routines of discussion for data presentation and corroboration. Data collection in the ethnographic mould is mandated to be open to checking and verification at each stage by other members of the research and scholarship community. Data in the ethnographic method is always gathered on the basis that it is open to "the checking up by others" (Mills, 1959, p. 126), though it is subject to the duty of care and ethical practice that the researcher has to their participants and their colleagues.

8.1   Subjective Biases

A criticism that is often remarked about qualitative methods of enquiry is that they are subjective and biased by the personal interpretations of the researcher. But as Boellstorff *et al* point out:

> "Subjectivity is an inescapable condition of science, no pure realm of objectivity exists in which the interests, biases, predilections, concerns, attitudes, dispositions, conceits, judgements, axioms, and presuppositions of investigators are absent and without impact. We always begin from somewhere" (Boellstorff et al., 2012, p. 41).

Such criticisms of qualitative studies supposed subjectivity misses the aim and the point of qualitative forms of study, as internal validity is not the primary concern of these forms of enquiry. The main thrust of the ethnographic method is towards *citation* and *accuracy*, tied with relevant *theoretical knowledge*, but most important, the narrative account that explains the links that are established between observation and theory.

The emphasis is on the *plausibility* and the *unambiguous form of the account*. In a sense qualitative forms of evidence and description are open to *criticism* rather than *proof* in the classical positivist sense.

The main evaluative frame of ethnographic research, then, is its *plausibility* and its *fit* with the knowledge community in which it is offered. This form of "post-positivist"(Kozinets, 2010, p. 162) evaluative framework is challenging, because, as Mills points out:

> "Classic social sciences [...] neither 'builds up' from microscopic study nor 'deduces down' from conceptual elaboration. Its practitioners try to build and to deduce at the same time, in the same processes of study, and to do so by means of adequate formulation and re-formulation of problems and of their adequate solutions" (Mills, 1959, p. 128).

Categories of evaluation, instead, are developed inductively as they emerge from the data collection process, and the narrative description process. They are not informed in advance. All of which makes them no less relevant or insightful if the data collection process is managed and verified as a formal process of fieldwork engagement. As Creswell notes:

> "In a qualitative methodology inductive logic prevails. Categories emerge from the informants, rather than are identified a priori by the researcher. This emergence provides rich 'context-bound' information leading to patterns or theories that help to explain a phenomenon" (Creswell, 1994, p. 7).

8.2   Local Knowledge

Ethnographic study is therefore about *building-up* a comparable and comprehensive body of knowledge that is grounded in context and is "infused with, and imbues, local knowledge's of the particular and specific" (Kozinets, 2010, p. 59). Ethnography does not offer universal generalisations, nor does it seek to establish universal patterns of data collection. Rather each investigative opportunity is uniquely built-up as an "adaptation of bricolage" that is "continually being refashioned to suit particular fields of scholarship, research questions, research sites, times, researcher preferences, skill sets, methodological innovations, and cultural groups" (Kozinets, 2010, p. 59). It is not uncommon in forms of ethnographic study for the researcher to be concerned with the "practical contingencies of people's lives." Indeed, undertaking an ethnographic study that has relevance to, and can offer strategies for, the practical concerns of the research participants is a clear motivating factor that should be reflected on by the researcher in their account. As Gail Miller suggests, the researcher's primary motive might be to "develop new strategies for responding to people's troubles and to construct social policies that take account of them" (Gale Miller in Miller & Dingwall, 1997, p. 3).

Whereas quantitative and normative research techniques might seek to "obtain answers to the same questions from a large number of individuals"(Bell, 2005, p. 14), the ethnographic researcher has to contend with the answers that are given by a relatively smaller number of people, being varied, contradictory and even incongruent. Thus, rather than seeing human behaviour as the product of a set of internal or external factors that acts on people and constitutes them as a medium through which these factors find expression (as subjects), qualitative research instead seeks to account for their accomplishments and interactions through meaning and through negotiation with other people, as a process (as agents).

9   Descriptive Accounts

Qualitative information, then, may take the form of reported and described accounts that are centred on the participants experience, rather than on statistical and calculative abstract comparative data sets. These experiences may be gained both in 'real-life' and through online and electronically mediated interaction. The ethnographic approach is interactionist, in that the object or unit of analysis consist, not of people as units, but rather of gestures, behaviours, acts and utterances that are shared and exchanged between people. The ethnographic investigator seeks to understand how the symbolic and communicative acts that are undertaken by different actors are performed, and what sense they make from them. As Robert Kozinets suggests in the context of computer mediated communication:

> "Every interactive online posting is a social action, a communicative performance that can be conceived of as a 'language game'. [And] if so, then every community 'player's' move in the social 'game' is a relevant observational event in and of itself" (Kozinets, 2010, p. 132).

This premise applies in all social communicative situations, be it in face-to-face interaction and/or in electronically mediated interaction. At this point it is sufficient to note that qualitative forms of research are more inclined to include a phenomenological rational because, as Creswell points out, the guiding principle of ethnography is

> "Based on the premise that human experience makes sense to those who live it, prior to all interpretations and theorising. Objective understanding is mediated by subjective experience itself, not constructed by an outside observer" (Creswell, 1998, p. 86).

This means that the two major objectives of ethnographic analysis, as previously noted, are to describe and analyse. The ethnographic researcher is seeking to understand the "processes through which social realities are constructed, and the social relationships through which people are connected to one another," because, as Gale Miller explains " it is within, and through, these relationships and processes that organisations, institutions, culture and society emerge and are sustained"(Gale Miller in Miller & Dingwall, 1997, p. 3).

9.1   Descriptive Accounts

Formulating a descriptive account of these realities, then, and the patterns of social relationship that they entail, is the task of the ethnographic researcher, and to do it in such a way that the account captures the many standpoints and interpretative implications or the different investigative techniques used. As Miller outlines in more detail:

> "Thus, both the descriptions of social reality that might be constructed by qualitative researchers, and the meanings that they might assign to the descriptions, vary depending on their observational and analytical position" (Gale Miller in Miller & Dingwall, 1997, p. 6).

By treating the emerging methodological choices as *standpoints*, rather than as fixed and immutable positions, it becomes possible to show how some of the interpretive possibilities of qualitative studies are established prior to data collection being undertaken. As Miller elaborates:

> "One way of conceptualising how qualitative researchers and their audiences are interrelated is by analysing them as members of interpretive communities. Such communities consist of shared orientations to social reality and interpretive practices that like-minded readers and writers bring to their reading and writing of texts. To say that interpretive community members are like-minded is not to say, however, that they are of one mind. Indeed, interpretative communities may involve diverse conflicts of interest and interpretation, but these conflicts are negotiated within contexts made up of community members' shared assumptions, concerns and interpretative practices" (Gale Miller in Miller & Dingwall, 1997, p. 8).

9.2   Interpretative Communities

The ethnographic researcher is writing, therefore, no less reflexively for their own *interpretative community*, such as they would expect the participants in their investigation to be thinking and acting reflexively within their community. The descriptive account is therefore an act of authorship through which the writer seeks to "produce detailed and situated accounts of specific cultures in a manner that reflects the perspective of those whose culture is under discussion" (Boellstorff et al., 2012, p. 14). These descriptive accounts are representative of the time that is spent in the field by the researcher, from their perspective, and might cover months or even years of work. They seek to describe the cultural patterns of the lived experience that has been shared by the participants, including the "mundane and routine" (Boellstorff et al., 2012, p. 21). As Robert Kozinets suggests, this act of authorship "is about struggling to transcend our own illusory categories and to understand the categories of the community and culture we are focussing upon"(Kozinets, 2010, p. 168). Moreover, "however this description is constructed it is the intense meaning of social life from the everyday perspectives of group members that is sought"(Kozinets, 2010, p. 59).

The experiences that are descriptively sought in contemporary ethnographic studies may often be found, and therefore best captured, in time-based multimedia formats. These formats are increasingly able to incorporate digital data collection techniques, including images, hypertext documents, video, audio, social media forums, message boards, chat rooms, personal media sites, blog sites, micro-blog sites, and other forms of electronic media. According to Robert Kozinets, the incorporation of multimedia and interactive forms of communication are legitimated within the descriptive account because they represent the social interactions of agents acting within a meaningful community. As such our assumption has to be that there are rules within this meaningful community that must be attended to by participants, and if there are rules then there are winner and losers.

Language and symbolic interaction is conceived in these situations as a gesture and a form of accomplishment that is played-out in meaningful ways, as a symbolic process of language game. Therefore all mediated representations can be treated as a social act because we can only make sense of these social acts in the "context of the appropriate social worlds" (Kozinets, 2010, p. 132) in which they take place. Keeping these definitions broad and non-exclusive is an ongoing challenge for the author of the descriptive account as the pressure to normalise and process-out any discrepancies is intense, either for academic convenience, or to meet professional practice standards. These routines of professional practice do not *in-themselves* give way *a priori* to useful investigation, however well-meaning and well-regarded they might be in the social settings that shape the institutional practice of ethnography. Reflexivity, therefore, is the key to ensuring that these descriptive accounts are valid and useful, even to the extent that they may challenge institutional norms.

10   Networks of Dependence

As much as anything else, then, ethnographic study comes to see individual actors, as Bauman & May suggest, "in terms of being members or partners in a network of interdependence." A network in which, and "regardless of what we do, we are dependent on others." The central question of sociology and ethnographic study, according to Bauman & May, therefore, is to ask:

> "How do the types of social relations and societies that we inhabit relate to how we see each other, ourselves and our knowledge, actions and their consequences" (Bauman & May, 2001, p. 5).

The ethnographic investigator who simply focuses on the gestures of the individuals and the "details of small-scale milieu" is not, according to Bauman and May, "putting his work outside the political conflicts and forces of his time." Instead, they are running the risk of "'accepting' the framework of his society" in an uncritical and unmethodical way.

In taking and using the methodological equipment of ethnographic study (and the social sciences more generally), the ethnographic investigator is able to equip themselves with the tools that will make it possible to envisage the wider social structure, and to make it "explicit and to study it as a whole" (Bauman & May, 2001, p. 78). The more proficient that ethnographic investigators become at organising data (as it is collected in this complex network of social relationships, gestures and acts), the better they will be at identifying the themes and ideas that are being articulated.

By asking relevant questions the social sciences hope to illuminate an understanding of otherwise complex and emergent social issues in the phenomenological tradition. It is important to remember, however, that this is a quest which seeks to find the *difference that makes the difference*, which by extension also asks "how do the practices of these branches of study differ from each other?" (Bauman & May, 2001, p. 4). Ethnographic study, as has been established earlier, is nothing without reflexive self-examination. The pragmatic nature of ethnographic methodology will be discussed in greater detail shortly, at this point it is sufficient to point out that driving the process of enquiry forward can be a general or a specific sense of doubt that the activities that we are engaged in are useful to us, and are able to help us to make sense of the world that we inhabit. As Richard Rorty states:

"It is a commonplace fact that people may develop doubts about what they are doing, and thereupon begin to discourse in ways incommensurable with those they used previously" (Rorty, 2009, p. 386).

Being able to articulate those doubts while maintaining good relationships within the networks of dependence that we inhabit is challenging. As meaning shifts and change, as resources are allocated to different tasks and for different purposes, as the traditions and inherited stocks of knowledge that we share between us become reified, the emergent languages of the curious investigator, or the rebellious upstart, becomes a fertile space for investigation, both because it allows us to glimpse and think about what can be maintained, and also what can be changed.

11   Theorising?

At this point it is worth making a brief note of the second aspect of qualitative investigation process that compliments the observational and descriptive mode of enquiry. This is the process of theorising. With the emphasis in qualitative research methods being based on multimodal, multi-perspectival and pragmatic data collection, there is a requirement in this approach for us to defer the development or application of any *strong* theoretical models. Ethnography, instead, seeks to delay the analysis of the collated data in a way that is retrospective, descriptive and reflexive. As Stephen Schensul *el al* suggest:

> "Ethnography does not test [a] formative theory to determine whether it is right or wrong. Instead it
>
> - Expands and fills the model
> - Discovers the qualitative and quantitative associations among domains or variables
> - Matches the expected results derived from the formative theory with the observed results that accrue from the data collection process" (Schensul et al., 1999 p.3).

It is considered useful that ethnographic studies develop a preliminary statement and working defence of its methodological approach, a justification that accounts for the *process* of modification as the *formative* ideas that are used in each of the stages, emerge. As part of this emergence these formative ideas are then merged with a set of *strong* ideas that are developed later, after the data has been reviewed, modelled and narrated. If we are to further heed advice from Mills about this, however, we should keep in mind that:

> "There is no 'grand theory', no one universal scheme in terms of which we can understand the unity of social structure, no one answer to the tired old problem of social order taken *uberhaupt* [in the first place]" (Mills, 1959, p. 46).

11.1   Sociological Thinking

In addition, and as Bauman and May point out, "thinking sociologically is a way of understanding the human world that also opens up the possibility for thinking about the same world in different ways" (Bauman & May, 2001, p. 5). We may encounter the same social phenomenon, but apply different forms of theory to it and come up with different levels and forms of analysis and recommendations. It is essential, then, that we recognise and delineate the different ways in which people perceive the social world through the blended and multimodal forms of ethnographic investigation techniques, and in the process, ask what different theories might be applied to offer a greater degree of validity or usefulness? For if we only see the world through a "singular glass" we will be unable to appreciate the "manifold perspectives" that might otherwise be distinguished (Shickman, 1978).

11.2   Building Theories

Further, in keeping with the inductive approach that was noted earlier as part of the data collection process, it will prove useful to maintain this style of thinking as we come to building theories based around the data we have collected. John Creswell suggests that it's not always possible to 'fit' a theory around a particular situation. The researcher should not be anticipating a neat fit between existing theory and observations, in the way that one might fit a 'container'' around a fluid. According to Creswell "one needs to build a new theory by using an inductive model of thinking or logic" (Creswell, 1994, p. 95). This makes writing from a theoretical point of view more difficult in an ethnographic study because, according to Creswell, "there is no standard terminology or rules about placement."

While the researcher may identify different theories and patterns of association in their data, there can be considerable variation between different types of study. And, because the design process for ethnographic research is site-specific, there are lower degrees of 'maturity' that might be applied to any associated theories and ideas. As a result, theorising is predominantly undertaken towards the end of the lifecycle of the analysis process. As Creswell notes "the placement of theory tends to be toward the end of the study" (Creswell, 1994, p. 101), which is much more arbitrary than it would be in more linear forms of social science. In some instances, the theory is introduced within an early literature review, in other instances theories are considered following the fieldwork and during the data analysis stage. However, as Robert Kozinets considers:

> "Inherent in the nature of ethnography [...] the researcher must constantly maintain a tension, taking back and community and culture, and the more abstract and distanced worlds of theory, words, generality, and research focus"(Kozinets, 2010, p. 97).

A critically oriented form of investigation may bank on its stock of theoretical and cultural concepts as they are associated with the literature survey, and so hinge on the internal scholarly community of academic readers to establish its rationale and field of action. As a result, it would feel natural in these circumstances to overextend the technical language of the theoretical discussion and to minimise the practical language and discussion based on the observations and practice that has been observed in the field. In turn, the observations and practice may best be understood in an anti-theoretical descriptive formulation, which depending on the primary discussing of those concepts, may only offer a limited set of references to the observed and participated subject matter.

11.3 Analytical Scaffolding

The security offered by undertaking the critical literature analysis first is clearly well regarded as an effective way to proceed with a research study, as it allows the researcher to *scaffold* in anticipation a set of ideas around the site and phenomenon. However, the risk is that the researcher is more focussed on *fitting* their observations into a pre-determined container of theory management, leaving them insensitive and ill-attuned to the emerging linkages, relationships and phenomena that might emerge from their chosen field or study. Thus, using theories to set the stage in an observational and participation driven study might be less productive than it might be in other forms of social science research. John Creswell ranks several issues that obscure and disrupt this fit between the established research practice, theory incorporation, and the observations drawn from the fieldwork. Creswell suggests that:

> "Characteristics of a qualitative research problem are: (a) the concept is 'immature' due to a conspicuous lack of theory and previous research; (b) the notion that the available theory may be inaccurate, incorrect, or biased; (c) a need exists to explore and describe the phenomena and to develop theory; or (d) the nature of the phenomenon may not be suited to quantitative measurements" (Creswell, 1994, p. 146).

The challenge for the ethnographic researcher, then, is to use theory sparingly and only when it is relevant as an act of symbolic accomplishment in itself; and instead focus on the actions and the contributions that people make in their social situations as a practical set of undertakings, responses and exchanges - as a set of accomplishments. Grounding the study in looking at what people do and say in their practical life-worlds is at the core of the ethnographic ethos. As Robert Kozinets points out:

> "Although evaluations and criteria are, ultimately, socially constructed, driven by consensus, and concerned with legitimacy and thus the exercise of power, they are nonetheless valuable and very difficult to dispense with"(Kozinets, 2010, p. 161).

12 Contingent Modelling

John Dewey reminds us that the "cultivation of a variety of alternative suggestions is an important factor in good thinking" (Dewey, 1910, p. 75). Dewey's pragmatic view impels a shift away from strong theories, for it is necessary to suggest an alternative process by which the wider, more generalised concerns that arise from ethnographic investigation, can be contextualised. Theories are convenient hooks and stories that help us to make sense of wider and more long-term social processes. They do not, *in-themselves*, however, drive actions, but instead help us to frame and justify our ethical assertions about the practical matters of living. Social theories are a language framework that attempts to offer scholarly communities a way to draw attention to contradictions and anomalies in the acknowledged social processes. They give people strength that the way that they are acting can be ethically justified, either for a higher purpose, or in order to challenge an established sense of principle.

As a mode of enquiry that covers a wide range of potential data forms from artefacts and interviews, to archival searchers, to content analysis and so on, it helps to think about the framework that this analysis will be expressed through. However, without recourse to grand narratives or trans-social explanations, the pragmatic turn impels the ethnographic process to come up with a different solution. This is where modelling proves itself useful. Modelling is contingent. It is dependent on the circumstances of the data analysis. It is linked to the purpose that it is being expeditiously used for. As Cohen, Manion and Morrison point out:

> "'Model' is sometimes used instead of or interchangeably with 'theory': 'Both may be seen as explanatory devices… though models are often characterised by the use of analogies to give a more graphic or visual representation of a particular phenomenon. Providing they are accurate and do not misrepresent the facts, models can be of great help in achieving clarity and focussing on key issues" (Cohen, Manion & Morrison 2000: 12-13 quoted in Bell, 2005, p. 102).

12.1   Heuristic Devices

A model is never meant to stand the test of time, nor is it able to generalise for all forms of social interaction. All a model does is provide a heuristic device for the analysis of a lone or sequential set of iterations of a narrative concept. Modelling is a reflexive proxy for the intangible, and as such it serves a practical purpose to help the researcher and the interpretative community in which they operate to make sense of the common terms, problems and issues associated with it. A model is not beyond criticism. It is not impermeable to creative and critical thought. It is a temporary analogy that is used to figure out if something functions or not. A model will help the researcher to understand and explain the interrelations that it is analogues to. As Boellstorff et al point out:

> "We cannot meaningfully 'pin down' the vastness of culture such that it can be parsed into separable variables controlled in experimental tests. As a peculiar and powerful adaptation to the problems of living and survival, culture has evolved as the most responsive, contingent, reflexive, and generative phenomenon that scientists have attempted to study. Our methods must be accountable to those properties of culture" (Boellstorff et al., 2012, p. 33).

12.2   Pragmatic Lived Experience

While the pragmatic turn does what it can to avoid grand social theory, there is still a clear need to establish a sense of "anticipatability, predictability and stability" (Schneider & Foot, 2005, p. 158) in the narrative and discursive accounts that are developed as a result of research practice and communication. For pragmatists, meaning, and hence creative action, is always found in the lived human context and situation. The question asked by pragmatists is, do we have the freedom to make something better out of the situations we find ourselves in? Will we be able to respond productively to new or different situations that we encounter? Can we find a better vocabulary to describe our experience than the one that is presently dominant? A pragmatist will thus avoid *theorising* (although theoretical jargon may never far from their lips), and will seek instead to *model* and to *map* the cultural and anthropological terrain based on evidence gathered from the field of enquiry.

In contrast to the positivistic empirical tradition, pragmatism says there are no theoretical starting points, only experiences and interpretations of social phenomena. For the pragmatist, to *model* is a better way of explaining social life, because it doesn't imply anything permanent, universalist or metaphysical. Local and temporary images are better valued than grand theories that purport to offer permanent or universal insight. And while modelling still retains connotations of theory, it gains a much higher degree of usefulness by simply relating useful stories that may offer some insight, and give some practical advantage, rather than building a whole world-view, system or ideology that can be universally imposed?

12.3   Developing Models

In a practical sense, then, it helps that the ethnographic researcher is able to develop models that link effectively between the data that has been collected and assumptions that need to be worked through in interpreting that data. Models are often difficult to build, but easy to discard. This is not a problem if it aids the creative process of interpretation by de-saturating the data and allowing any extraneous content to be side-lined (or even the opposite in some cases). Moreover, models lack the dispassionate objectivism of more classical forms of social theory management, though instead they do allow for a more creative engagement with the subject matter. They are useful for plotting courses that go beyond the core assumptions of the host knowledge community, as John Creswell explains:

> "Data analysis requires that the researcher be comfortable with developing categories and making comparisons and contrasts [i.e. modelling]. It also requires that the researcher be open to possibilities and see contrary or alternative explanations for the findings" (Creswell, 1994, p. 153).

This close affinity between collecting data and offering interpretations is carefully managed in the "traditional linear method of proceeding," because it allows the "researcher not only to ask the following question repeatedly but also to answer it:

- How far do the methods, categories, and theories that are used do justice to the subject and the data?" (Flick, 2009, p. 92).

Modelling, therefore, is an adequate response to the data that the ethnographic researcher collects, and usefully draws them away from the hang-ups and cul-de-sacs that are possible when attempting to *get a theory to work*.

13   What Do People Do?

The foundational concept of ethnographic observation, then, is to consider what people *do*, and in doing what they do, how these *acts of accomplishment* might be perceived as *meaningful* in different social contexts and through different acts of negotiation? These are acts of symbolic importance to which the ethnographic investigator must be attuned and able to relate. All social and cultural acts or utterances have a function and serve a communicative purpose. All social and cultural acts or utterances have symbolic value and therefore are understood or interpreted within familiar or unfamiliar frameworks of conversation or reference. As Zygmunt Bauman and Tim May suggest:

> "From this point of view we can say that [ethnography] is distinguished through viewing human actions as elements of wider figurations: mutual dependency (dependency being a state in which the probability that the action will be undertaken and the chance of its success change in relation to what other actors are, do or may do). Sociologists ask what consequences this has for human actors, the relations into which we enter and the societies of which we are a part" (Bauman & May, 2001, p. 5).

The focus here, then, is to consider actions and relationships as inherently meaningful within the context of human group life, not as distanced and impartial observers, but from close proximity and with affinity. According to this approach the researcher accepts that we are social beings who's existence only makes sense in the context of a social life, and therefore will only be served well by attempting to understand the ways that people make sense of their experiences and how they "construct meaningful activities in their daily worlds" (Kathy Charmaz in Prus, 1996, p. xii). This is a view of human existence that is fundamentally social, and which calls on us to understand the way that we interact with others from within our social groups. The ethnographic investigator is reflecting on the way that our interpretations of our social interactions with others are regulated and shaped. The world of social and cultural interaction is diffuse and ephemeral, and therefore it necessitates a sensitivity on the part of the investigator to recognise that different interpretations are possible from similarly shared experiences. As Kathy Charmaz notes,

> "At essence, we are social beings. We interact within society and are influenced by our interpretations of our interactions with others. We strive to develop shared definitions of our worlds and of our experiences with these others" (Kathy Charmaz in Prus, 1996, p. xii).

13.1 Practices of Daily Life

This *intersubjectivity*, as it is championed by Robert Prus, is an *accomplishment*, or an act of *doing*, which takes place in the mundane practices of our daily lives. We construct and reconstruct meanings from these actions and from the utterances that we enact and encounter. As described by Charmaz, Prus "views intersubjectivity explicitly as an on-going *accomplishment*. Thus, reality is not given; nor is it entirely predictable. In contrast, Prus argues that people together construct and reconstruct meaning, as they act and interact. Essentially then, meanings arise, are maintained, and change as people pursue daily activity" (Kathy Charmaz in Prus, 1996, p. xiii).

13.2 Technology

It is worth making a brief note at this point about the role that technology plays as a mediating concept in the process of social interaction and community maintenance. As technology is dominant structuring concept within our cultural lives, often regarded as pervasive and all encompassing. It is quite often said that we are living in, what Robert Kozinets calls, an "age of 'technosociality.'" An age in which "individuals and communities are situated to various extents in delocalised information networks [that] constitute social relationships through technocultural processes" (Kozinets, 2010, p. 171). The role that technology plays in the social and intersubjective relationships cannot go unnoticed by the ethnographic researcher, who has to either accept this assertion at face value, adding it as just another form of determinism that has to be rooted out; or, instead, the ethnographer can challenge this determination and look for the ways in which technology is understood and accommodated as an accomplishment in the daily lives of people acting and living in communities. As Kozinets suggest:

> "The insight that technology does not determine culture, but that they are co-determining, co-constructive forces, is a crucially important one. With our ideas and actions, we choose technologies, we adapt and shape them. To this realisation it is also critical to add that our culture does not entirely control the technologies that we use, either. The way that technology and culture interact is a complex dance, and interweaving and intertwining"(Kozinets, 2010, p. 22).

Therefore, when it comes to the analyses the social relationships that are found in every-day practice, it is incumbent on the researcher to make space in the data collection process, and the narrative analysis model that gets written, for the role and purpose of technology. As Christine Hine suggests:

> "Our knowledge of the new technologies would be shaped in significant ways by the methods through which we choose to know them and the underlying epistemological commitments on which those methods rely" (Hine, 2005, p. 7).

As a reflexive process, therefore, the ethnographic investigation not only accounts for technology, but also offers insight into the way that technology is symbolically represented in the practices and accomplishments of the communities that are being studied.

14   Ethnography and Experience

According to John Creswell "The focus of qualitative research is on participants' perceptions and experiences, and the way they make sense of their lives. The attempt is to understand not one, but multiple realities" (Creswell, 1994 p.163). As such, then, ethnographic research techniques are a mechanism by which we are able to identify and map the 'processes' that underpin the relationships within a social situation. These are processes that either separate or bind people together; or, that serve to distribute legitimacy to the meanings that are shared and understood in different social contexts, and by different social actors. Ethnographic study offers a 'view' on how these things work, and in what way they may be adapted or challenged, in order that they might influence an alternative outcome. However, in doing this, ethnographic study also seeks to avoid generalisations, and declines to offer 'universal' political metanarratives or truths. As McCarthy and Wright point out

> "The ethnographic turn is generally seen as a turn away from the possibility of neutral description. There can be no literal interpretation of the logic of other people's sense making, and certainly there can be no transliteration from their way of making sense to ours" (McCarthy & Wright, 2004 p.36).

Qualitative research is therefore shaped by the assumption that it is an "emergent design in its negotiated outcomes", and as such, "meanings and interpretations are negotiated with human data sources because it's the subjects' realities that the researcher attempts to reconstruct" (Creswell, 1994 p.163).

14.1   Feeling and Intuition

The ethnographic approach relies on our ability to narrate the 'feeling' and the 'intuition' we have for meaning. Ethnography acknowledges that our commonly used techniques for social understanding always cross artificial academic/disciplinary boundaries and traditions of formal thinking. Ethnography is mindful that social actors have to deal with 'multiple realities' that are played out within contested and constrained circumstances, and that the data that is produced in these conditions would not otherwise form a 'quantifiable' evaluation in the general terms of the positivist or quantitative tradition. The dataset that is produced through qualitative techniques is instead more 'worldly' and more bounded by experience. As John Creswell continues:

> "Objectivity and truthfulness are critical to both research traditions. However, the criteria for judging a qualitative study differ from quantitative research. First and foremost, the researcher seeks believability based on coherence, insight and instrumental utility and trustworthiness through a process of verification rather than through traditional validity and reliability measures" (Creswell, 1994 p.163).

Added to this, and as McCarthy and Wright suggest (in relation to their study of the role and impact of technology on people's lives), we should be open to thinking in "terms of the felt life and the felt emotional quality of action and interaction" (McCarthy & Wright, 2004 p.12). These subjective and interpretive qualities are often missed in quantitative forms of research, but which can be given priority in more qualitative methodologies and operations. As Uwe Flick argues:

> "The essential features of qualitative research are the correct choice of appropriate methods and theories; the recognition and analysis of different perspectives; the researchers' reflections on their research as part of the process of knowledge production; and the variety of approaches" (Flick, 2009 p.14).

14.2   Verification and Reliability

An obvious question at this stage, then, is to ask on what basis this data and information can be relied, and to what extent is it open to verification? If ethnographic investigation draws on subjective personal experiences and contextual interpretations, what mechanisms can be generally applied that will ensure that readers of a study can vouch for its veracity? One answer, as Creswell notes, is the diversity of sources and recording techniques used to capture it. For Creswell "unquestionably, the backbone of qualitative research is extensive collection of data, typically from multiple sources of information" (Creswell, 1998 p.19). It is assumed here, then, that by adopting this particular approach, that the multiplicity of data collection and recording techniques will be a *de facto* operational characteristic, and that the movement between different types of data collection technique will be interchangeable and fluid (blended), on the basis that this will aid the storytelling and narrative process. Consequently, these stories are focused on the experiences of the participants in the study. As

Robert Kozinets reminds us "ethnography is grounded in context; it is infused with, and imbues, local knowledge's of the particular and specific"(Kozinets, 2010, p. 59). The challenge of the ethnographic researcher is to structure and write an account of the experiences of the participants so that the context is clear, and the concepts are pertinent. As Uwe Flick comments:

> "Whether the picture that is formed in this way is true or correct cannot be determined. But its quality may be assessed through its viability; that is, the extent to which the picture or model permits the subject to find its way and to act in the world" (Flick, 2009, p. 71).

14.3 Relationships and Experience

Experience is thus a process of social interchange in which our relationships as agents in various overlapping life-worlds are held and mediated through language (symbolic exchange), which in turn sets the scene and helps us to comprehend the social function of our relationships. As Flick points out "the eventualities of the social process involved have an influence on what will survive as a valid or useful explanation" (Flick, 2009, p. 71). Facts are not waiting *out-there* for the researcher to stumble across them in an act of discovery. Instead facts emerge from the interchange of roles, positions, dramatic modes of behaving, and the numerous other forms of symbolic interchange that we can account for. As Flick explains, this form of social constructivism is "the point of departure for research" because the "ideas of social events, of things or facts which we meet in a social field under study, and the way in which these ideas communicate with one another (i.e. compete, conflict, and succeed) are shared and taken for real"(Flick, 2009, p. 76).

Likewise, and as John Creswell notes, "for the qualitative researcher, the only reality is that constructed by the individuals involved in the research situation" (Creswell, 1994, p. 4). Therefore, the emphasis given to experience in the ethnographic model of research is central. Subsequently, however, it does make the forming of a narrative that explains those experiences that much more difficult. Either we can seek out an approach to social analysis that is low-risk and without ambiguity or frustration, or we develop a set of practices and templates for the study of subjective experience "in which the 'rules' and procedures are not fixed, but rather are open and emerging" (Creswell, 1994, p. 9). The ethnographic researcher, therefore, in thinking about and attempting to account for these subjective experiences is advised to "'follow the people', 'follow the metaphor', and 'follow the artefact.'" In other words, the ethnographic researcher is encouraged to pursue "sites of investigation" that are in "dynamic dialogue" and which allow us to "trace linkages between them" by "attempting to establish and explain critical interrelations" (Boellstorff et al., 2012, p. 59). In short, it is the privilege of the ethnographic researcher to transliterate these enunciations of social experience and meaning.

14.4 Meaning Making

Ethnography, then, draws on theories of meaning that prefigure *action*, *experience* and *participation* as the primary sources of reference to the social construction of meaning. But ethnography also seeks to temper these impulses with a reflexive imperative, based on observation and empirical validation (Amit, 2000; Davis,

1999). Meaning, in the ethnographic tradition, is seen as a culturally situated process that is made by people participating in communities. Meaning is something that is gained in and through conversation, which is shot-through with personal values and personal biases. According to Robert Prus

> "Ethnographers find themselves attempting to come to terms with (i) the perspectives or worldviews characterising the people in the settings in which they find themselves, (ii) the sets of self and other identities that people in those settings invoke, (iii) the activities that take place in those arenas, (iv) the relationships that develop between the participants in those life-worlds, (v) the emotionalities that people in those contexts express, and (vi) their modes of achieving communicative fluency" (Prus, 1997 p.20).

In ethnography meaning is intensely personal and emotional. Meaning is never fixed but changes and only lives within the contingent conditions within which it is described by subjects. In ethnography there is no objective position or vantage point from which the researcher can observe meaning in action. Indeed, as Pierre Bourdieu points out:

> "In taking up a point of view on the action, withdrawing from it in order to observe it from above and from a distance, he [the researcher] constitutes practical activity as an object of observations and analysis, a representation" (Bourdieu, 1977 p.2).

The significance of which is that the process of making ethnographic research *itself* has to be accounted for in the practice of any study, as this process of *becoming engaged and attuned* to these meanings is itself a significant contributing factor in the accumulation of the data. Reflection is as significant as any other source of information, interpretative process or process of codification. Bourdieu goes on to argues that:

> "It is not sufficient for anthropology [and therefore social study] to break with native experience and the native representation of that experience: it has to make a second break and question the presuppositions inherent in the position of an outside observer" (Bourdieu, 1977 p.2).

14.5   Reflexive Impulse

This second break in the representation of experience recognises, moreover, that the observer has *inherited* and *locally arrived* at the position that they presently occupy. For social constructivists this helps to clear away some of the contradictions that might otherwise arise in trying to tie-up the ethnographic process too neatly, and without due attention to the reflexive impulse. The temptation might be to pronounce this observational break as circular, regressive and teleological, as it might be said that there is a risk that any of the observer's comments may be liable to fall-in on themselves, under the weight of self-referential elasticity. As a negative test of validity, however, this is only applicable if our aim is to produce a neutral, hygienically monitored and hermetic observational practice.

The social constructivist works with a different form of appraisal to hand, and would rather assess and evaluate social phenomena on the basis that they emerge *unfinished*, *incomplete* and in a state of *disorder*, from the ecologies and environments of the real world. Uwe Flick cites Herbert Blumer's three steps for establishing coherence in the observational process:

"The first premise is that human beings act toward things on the basis of the meanings that the things have for them… The second premise is that the meaning of such things is derived from, or arises out of, the social interaction that one has with one's fellows. The third premise is that these meanings are handled in, and modified through, an interpretive process used by the person in dealing with the things he encounters"(Blumer, 1967 quoted in Flick, 2009, p. 58).

The extent, then, to which the ethnographic researcher can write a plausible account of the interpretative framework that has been built-up between the participants, is about as much as we can expect from the whole process. As has already been indicated, this is an issue of *validity* rather than *proof.*

14.6   Situational Meanings

Different people ascribe different meanings in different situations. The events may be the same, but the accounts of those events may vary. Conflict between the holders of these different views is all too common, as they compete with each other to assert their version of the story that asserts their identity. As Boellstorff *et al* suggest "different versions of the same story can be highly informative, illustrating the many facets of how individuals view a collective phenomenon" (Boellstorff et al., 2012, p. 97). To what extent will a symbolic model or picture that a social actor has in their mind help them to find their way and to act in the world? To what extent do these actors ascribe 'truth' to these stories, and how central is the concept of 'truthfulness' to the whole enterprise of social identity for that social group or subculture? In the social constructionist model our experience is structured through concepts such as 'truth,' so it is no surprise that when we actually observe people acting naturally in their intimate and familiar social environments, what they do is not necessarily what they have said that they do.

As Boellstorff *et al* suggest, "this concern harks back to Malinowski's famous distinction between what people do and what they say they do" (Boellstorff et al., 2012, p. 87). There is an inherent fluidity and dynamic interchange in the way that people generate, negotiate, store and expend meanings in practical usage. As Boellstorff *et al* continue, "people and culture are emergently, dynamically constituted, constantly shifting, alternately undergoing periods of destabilisation and stabilisation" (Boellstorff et al., 2012, p. 35). Therefore:

"While there is an important difference between people's speech and action, this does not mean that what people say they do is insignificant. The meanings people give to their actions and the world around them form and essential component of understanding. Interviews provide opportunities to learn about people's elicited narratives and representations of their social worlds, including beliefs, ideologies, justifications, motivations, and aspirations. These are part of any culture. They are emphatically not epiphenomenal or second-order artefacts of an underlying social order; they are part and parcel of that social order and this have causal power" (Boellstorff et al., 2012, p. 93).

The focus of the ethnographic study, then, is to establish the contingent themes of this social interchange, and to look for the patterns of knowledge that bear significance. What are the concepts that regulate this interchange and how are they used? What are these concepts and forms of knowledge that empower actors in their beliefs that they can act and accomplish things? As Flick explains:

> "Knowledge is constructed in processes of social interchange; it is based on the role of language in such relationships; and, above all, it has social functions. The eventualities of the social process involved have an influence on what will survive as a valid or useful explanation" (Flick, 2009, p. 71).

Thus, people spend their time solving problems and making meanings, they access systems of support and community/identity empowerment, they arrange their lives so that they have access to a "flexible repertoire of resources." It is the role of the ethnographer, therefore, to look at how those "systems of support [are] anchored in culture." As Boellstorff *et al* highlight:

> "We organise ethnographic investigation so that we can access the complex arrangements by which people solve problems and make meanings. Our work has a high degree of validity because we directly observe and interact with what we want to know; we do not wrench phenomena out of their contexts, thereby rendering them uninterpretable" (Boellstorff et al., 2012, p. 38).

14.7   Multiple Connections

At the end of the day, then, ethnographic research highlights the multiple connections between different social phenomena. There is a connection between one social phenomenon and many other social phenomena. The task of the ethnographic researcher is to guide and to explain those connections, to thread through their contradictions and to alleviate the confusion that is commonplace when so much is *buzzing* at one time. Human "communication is the exchange of meaningful symbols, and all manner of human symbol systems are being [shared]" (Kozinets, 2010, p. 8). These acts are meaningful, not only as a transaction between individuals, but also as a way of learning what it means to be a member or a contributor to a community. These acts never take place in isolation, because they ultimately can only be understood in a shared community of language and meaning. As John Creswell highlights, the design process of ethnographic research is one that uses, both implicitly and explicitly:

> "A set of philosophical assumptions that guide the study. These assumptions speak to our understanding of knowledge: Knowledge is within the meanings people make of it; knowledge is gained through people talking about their meanings; knowledge is laced with personal biases and values; knowledge is written in a personal, up-close way; and knowledge evolves, emerges, and is inextricably tied to the context in which it is studied" (Creswell, 1998, p. 19).

One potential, and tentative definition to emerge from this process, therefore, is that a community and social life can be thought of as a *symbolic* and *practical* space in which our meanings are *congruent*.

15   Ethnography and Pragmatism

Framing this discussion and set of observations about the practice of ethnographic study and the social sciences, moreover, has been a set of debates that Robert Prus characterises as being "between the positivists and the interpretivists" (Prus, 1996, p. 3). According to Prus "over the past century, the social sciences have been dominated by 'positivist' (structuralist) approaches to the study of human behaviour" (Prus, 1996, p. 2). The impact of which, according to Prus, has been to narrow the field of study and to restrict the legitimacy of forms of enquiry that go beyond the instrumental and the quantifiable. Raising questions about this restriction of thought, according to Prus, are the pragmatist thinkers, most commonly associated with William James, John Dewey, Charles Sanders Peirce, and Richard Rorty, as well as cultural anthropologists Margaret Mead, Ralph Bulmer and Herbert Blumer. According to Prus:

> "The pragmatists' emphases were somewhat diverse, but they were generally opposed to 'rationalist' or 'determinist' (i.e., positivist) philosophy and wanted to develop conceptualisations of human behaviour that attended to the actualities and practices of people" (Prus, 1996, p. 46).

Sharing a common objective to find ways to describe and understand how social life is *lived* and *experienced*, the pragmatic ethos promotes alternative notions of how improvements to the human condition can be brought about on a practical level. And so they "begin to attend to the socially constituted (and relativistic) nature of human group life."

15.1   Agency and Communication

Rather than conceiving of social groups as a mass or as a machine, the pragmatist attitude considers how people can be understood as "reflective beings who possessed capacities to act mindfully of their own situations and in conjunction with others" (Prus, 1996, p. 47). This is a model of human behaviour that foregrounds *human agency* and *communication*, while at the same time mapping out ideas about how social processes enable and support those intersubjective acts. It has been intimated a number of times in this paper already, that central to the ethnographic method is the pragmatic principle which says that *objects by themselves have no meaning, but when they are constituted and used as part of a system of communication they are socially constituted with meaning*. The question that is asked in the pragmatist tradition, therefore, is how do people develop the manners and the repertoires of meaning that brings about their association with those meanings? Where do meanings come from as part of the social interchange of community life? Where does the meaningful sense of 'self' arise in community life? What form, and to what purpose, does our language support or facilitate these meanings in practical usage? Pragmatism seeks to avoid reference to externalised social concepts or metanarrative, be they historical, philosophical or political, and instead concerns itself with "the study of group life 'in the making,'" i.e. the different ways that people do things, and the different ways that people "make sense of and act towards [things]" (Prus, 1999, p. 125).

Richard Rorty advocated the 'pragmatisation' of the social sciences, and contested the limits of social and philosophical theory. Rorty argued that "If we see knowledge [i.e. meaning] as a matter of conversation and of social practice, rather than as an attempt to mirror nature, we will not be likely to envisage a meta-practice which will be the critique of all possible social practice" (Rorty, 2009 p.171). Rorty advocated, instead, that what is important about our shared social lives are the continuous conversations that build-up between participants who form and build a community, as opposed to the attempt to build a unifying structure or metanarrative that would otherwise explain people's lives. The use of language that is legitimated through emerging vocabularies, and then confirmed in established vocabularies, is rich ground, according to Rorty, for social enquiry, and as such, these are the processes of conversational change that ought to be mapped out in social or cultural study. As Rorty argues

> "The notion of culture as a conversation rather than as a structure erected upon foundations fits well with the hermeneutical notion of knowledge, since getting into a conversation with strangers is like acquiring a new virtue or skill by imitating models" (Rorty, 2009 p.319).

15.2 Trans-Social Ascription

A central part of this pragmatic way of thinking, then, asserts that we can more usefully think about *modelling* the behaviours and experiences of participants in communities, rather than imposing external social structures on them, or ascribing trans-social forces that give a neat and tied-together explanation. For Rorty the challenge is to listen to the conversations at hand in order to map out the *commensurable* and the *incommensurable* components of the language and culture of the participants. The premise of this argument asserts that shifts are always taking place in the expectations, beliefs and experiences of the practitioners of different communities, and that these shifts are giving way to more dynamic and dispersed social environments and sets of social relationships (some of which are technically embedded, and others which are not). Therefore, a pragmatic ethnographic study of an emergent community of participants might be thought of as an "attempt to reinterpret our familiar surroundings in the unfamiliar terms of our new inventions" (Rorty, 2009 p.360).

So, in focussing on participants within a selected community, it will be possible to represent and locate this environment as a *symbolic social space* in which this tension between familiarity (the *commensurable*) and strangeness (the *incommensurable*) is played out. Robert Kozinets describes this approach in relation to ethnographic practice when he describes how:

> "Neo-pragmatic validity places dissensus, heterogeneity and discourse in the foreground, destabilising the author's position as master of truth and knowledge. This dissensus and multivocal orientation comes somewhat naturally to the online community environment, with its cacophony of contending voices. Reflexivity reminds us not to smooth over conflicts and differences in our analysis and research representation, but to accurately convey"(Kozinets, 2010, p. 170).

This represents, then, an opportunity for enquiry that allows for a specific series of questions to be asked about what the motivating factors are for participating in community life, and how they are understood by participants when sharing and conversing? This means listening to and accounting for the manner in which these participants comprehend the network of relationships that exist between themselves and different actors who are engaged in activities associated with them. Likewise, we might also ask, to what extent will those activities that are perceived as either *macro* or *micro* priorities play a role and with what effect? In other words, how do participants in these our chosen communities make sense of the phenomenon that shape their personal expectations? As a community of practice perhaps (Wenger, 1998)? As a community of identity? As a language community? As a community of interest? Crucially, this means tracking and identifying the forms of language that participants use when they communicate, interact and justify their activities? But, it also means

that the researcher has to consider what the boundaries are between the different concepts that participants
define and use?

In short, how do participants comprehend these activities and circumstances as they have changed over time;
with the introduction of new communication techniques, and against the backdrop of changing perceptions of
success and failure, or esteem and reward? Emphasis should be placed, therefore, on narrowing the terms of
the research by specifically following the 'actors' in tightly defined situations. And in keeping with this pragmatic ethos, a practical research methodology will avoid hints of grand schemes or willingness to find evidence
of 'critical challenge' within the emerging practices and vocabularies. A pragmatic ethnography will instead
look for descriptions of *resonant strategies*, *role playing*, *modelling* and *sense making* that help participants to
engage in the changing social circumstances. Ultimately, the pragmatic approach encourages research that
isn't hindered by theories of historical or large scale ecological/political change. The task of ethnographic investigation, we should remember, is not to prove or disprove facts and hypothesis, but instead to weigh the
ideas that are given *repute* and *validation* in a social setting – in other words, to offer commentary on what
can be *credited* and what can be *discredited*. As Bell quotes Langeveld:

> "Many researchers in areas such as education, social science and health are directly concerned with
> the practical outcomes of research and in particular, the improvement of practice in their organisa-
> tion. The aim is not only 'to know facts and to understand relations for the sake of knowledge. We
> want to know and understand in order to be able to act and act 'better' than we did before'"(Lange-
> veld 1965: 4 quoted in Bell, 2005, p. 28).

15.3   Ethnography and Lived Experience

In community life, like ethnographic study, credibility doesn't come from being a sceptic; instead it comes from
being a participant. If the goal of ethnographic investigations is to document the "conflicting perspectives on
media change rather than to critique them" (Jenkins, 2006 p.133), then it is desirable to take solidly social constructivist and pragmatic approaches. These approaches will be multimodal and multi-perspectival in their
form, and will seek to establish the patterns of lived experience that participants enact and enunciate. C.
Wright Mills suggests:

> "The sociological imagination [...] in considerable part consists of the capacity to shift from one per-
> spective to another, and in the process to build up an adequate view of a total society and of its com-
> ponents" (Mills, 1959, p. 211).

And as we build this view of the society in which we are engaging with, and its constituent components, then it
will be advantageous to seek to understand the basis of the wide and varied experiences that we can draw
upon. For example, it is often said that we are living in an era of extensive social change empowered by ICT
and social media technologies, and that these technologies are facilitating and providing enhanced capability
for the extension of many of the established communicative practices that we had previously been familiar
with. Don Tapscott argues, for example, that "Web 2.0 makes it easier for ordinary people to organise

themselves, instead of having to do so under the control of hierarchical, often authoritarian, organisation" (Tapscott, 2008 p.40). If this is the case, at what point is it appropriate for students and researchers of these social phenomenon to try to account for, and reflect on, the characteristics of the associated intersubjective communities that are intertwined with them? As John McCarthy and Peter Wright suggest, a "pragmatist philosophy of experience is particularly clarifying with respect to experience."

According to McCarthy and Wright, pragmatism "sees knowledge as participative" and therefore dependent on the "circumstances, situation and actions from which it was constructed" (McCarthy & Wright, 2004 p.17). For pragmatist social commentators meaning is accrued when we veer away from positivistic epistemologies, and instead recognise that it is "knowledge in a community of engaged people, in a situation, from a perspective, felt, and sens[ual]" that we ought to pay attention. As McCarthy and Wright continue:

> "For pragmatists, therefore, knowing, doing, feeling, and making sense are inseparable. Pragmatism is a practical, consequential philosophy, a practice that is concerned with imagining and enriching as much as understanding. The test it sets for itself is to improve things" (McCarthy & Wright, 2004 p.17).

Experience, as it is situated in the life-worlds of the participants we seek to engage with, is therefore the central process for this form of enquiry. These are not lifeworld experiences that are *grand* or *overarching*; but instead consists of what C Wright Mills calls the "many little causes," those acts that are scattered as fragments within their milieux. For Mills, we, the "social scientists of milieux" must act as "practical men," and aim to be "piecemeal reformers of milieux, one here one there" (Mills, 1959, p. 86). As Mills elaborates:

> "When we understand social structures and structural changes as they bear upon more intimate scenes and experiences, we are able to understand the causes of individual conduct and feelings of which men in specific milieux are themselves unaware" (Mills, 1959, p. 162).

15.4　Intimate Experiences

So, it is to these intimate scenes of experience that the ethnographer has to be attuned. If the researcher is focussed on the search for great social structures or historical forces, it means that they may well be witness to a great many radical ideas and actions, but because they do not serve their predetermined ends, then they might write them off as being merely irrational or peripheral. The mundane experience of everyday living means, as Mills points out, that "ordinary men often cannot reason about the great structures – rational and irrational – of which their milieux are subordinate parts" (Mills, 1959, p. 168). It is the job of the social scientists, therefore, as Mils point out, to:

> "Examine trends in an effort to answer the questions 'where are we going?' – and that is what social scientists are often trying to do. In doing so, we are trying to study history rather than to retreat into it, to pay attention to contemporary trends without being 'merely journalistic,' to gauge the future of these trends without being merely prophetic" (Mills, 1959, p. 153).

Furthermore, for Mills, the:

> "Implications for our methods seem clear and simple: the selection of milieux for detailed study ought
> to be made in accordance with problems of structural significance. The kinds of 'variables' to be iso-
> lated and observed within milieux ought to be those that have been found to be important by our ex-
> amination of structure. The development of social science cannot very well be thought of as resulting
> from a scattered group of women each making a part of some great quilt" (Mills, 1959, p. 69).

In this context, then, the pursuit of structure has a particular meaning. It is structuring as a *process* rather than as a *force* that allows us to focus on the *acts* and *accomplishments*, the *intersubjective* patterns that are the regulating patterns which emerge in the indeterminate spaces of negotiation between individuals acting in communities. We are individuals who communicate and exchanging thoughts, ideas, roles, identities, tasks, rules, and so on, on a day-to-day basis, with little regard to ideologies, metanarratives or hegemonic social structures. This form of intersubjective structuring is not an externalised form of structure, as a class conflict, or a division between material conditions (though no doubt those ways of thinking about social relationships have a notable effect on our perception of social realities). Instead, these are, as Mills points out, "historical transformations [that] carry meanings not only for individual ways of life, but for the very character – the limits and possibilities of the human being" (Mills, 1959, p. 158). The job of the ethnographic researcher, then, is to focus on experience, and those forms of experience that are reported by actors who are engaged in the day-to-day of community life. For as Mills notes, it is the social scientists role to:

> "Try to understand men and women as historical and social actors, and the ways in which the variety
> of men and women are intricately selected and intricately formed by the variety of human societies"
> (Mills, 1959, p. 225).

It is, however, the job of men and women to live their lives and do the best that they can given the circum-stances and the symbolic and practical tools that they have to hand.

15.5   Ethnography and Identity

Drawing on the ideas of Erving Goffman and his concept of the dramaturlurgical, it is worth reflecting on how the concept of *identity performance* might be useful in helping the ethnographic researcher to manage the analysis of individuals presenting themselves in their social milieu and engaging with others. As an empirical tool, the premise that individuals 'perform' their sense of belonging to different communities is rich. Goffman suggests that, as Guimaraes explains, "in every context of social life actors play different roles consistent with the respective contexts that are dynamically negotiated with other actors" (Guimaraes, 2005, p. 153). The eth-nographer is interested in establishing a plausible narrative about how we maintain our social relationships. Furthermore, the way that individual manage multiple forms of identity as social actors, is a useful way to think about the social/symbolic context for our sense being in a community, and our sense of belonging as the situations that are engaged in change. As Goffman argues:

> "The self, then, as a location whose fundamental fate is to be borne, to mature, and to die, it is a dra-
> matic effect arising diffusely from a scene that is presented, and the characteristic issue, the crucial
> concern, is whether it will be credited or discredited"(Goffman, 1990, p. 245).

Robert Prus takes up Goffman's concept of dramatology and its use in the everyday accomplishment of identity expression, particularly the way that identities are shaped, presented and negotiated. According to Prus:

> "Goffman portrays in strikingly vivid detail the ways which people take images of themselves and others into account in constructing their day-to-day interchanges with one another" (Prus, 1996, p. 80).

These ways of thinking about identity view culture in *process terms*, a process in which we articulate our sense of identity in the *flow of social exchanges* and as a mechanism for establishing, building and *maintaining social relationships*. As Guimares points out, culture is not "homogeneous or fixed as the upshot of established traditions, but is continuously in motion and subject to change." Which makes the performances and social practices of local communities an "appropriate empirical element" (Guimaraes, 2005, p. 144). For the individual to be able to express, confirm or challenge their sense of identity in a sincere way they "must behave according to the environment's meaning framework," and in doing so they reveal something about the "culture of the group" (Guimaraes, 2005, p. 153). For as Mills reminds us, "the life of an individual cannot be adequately understood without reference to the institutions within which his biography is enacted" (Mills, 1959, p. 161). And if we are to understand the identities that we encounter, then we also have to understand the institutions and settings that they are connected with. As Mills explains:

> "The view of man as a social creature enables us to go much deeper than merely the external biography as a sequence of social roles. Such a view requires us to understand the most internal and 'psychological' features of a man: in particular, his self-image and his conscience and indeed the very growth of his mind" (Mills, 1959, p. 161).

The broad range of regulating processes in social life, of which identity is one, are rich and fertile ground for ethnographic research, and add to the potential for additional engagement in the field.

16   Methodological Objectives

What is regarded as the defining characteristic of the ethnographic approach, and which differentiates it from other aligned forms of qualitative research, is participant observation. As Boellstorff *et al* summarise:

> "One method above all others is fundamental to ethnographic research. This method is participant observation, the cornerstone of ethnography. Participant observation is the embodied emplacement of the researching self in a fieldsite as a consequential social actor. We participate in everyday life and become well known to our informants. If a methodological toolbox does not include participant observation, the approach may be legitimate and effective for exploring a number of topics, but it is not ethnographic. Through participant observation, ethnographers step into the social frame in which activity takes place" (Boellstorff et al., 2012, p. 65).

This somewhat extended tour of the ethnographic method so far, has been a way of demonstrating how the threads of the ethnographic method intertwine together and become pertinent to the process of investigation, not only as an observer, but also as a participant in the field.

The routines and roles that are played out by people going about their daily lives can be understood only within the accomplishments of daily life. *Experience, identity, meaning* and *active accomplishments* (doing) are all facets of the daily routines of our lives. The extent to which we may wish to participate in the daily life of our communities is to some extent, though not in all ways, unique to us all. However, and regardless of the limitations of our interactions, we have to do so on the basis that *experience, identity, meaning* and the *accomplished actions* that we undertake, are all part of the available range of *generic social processes* that we can call on. These contributions can be both a positive and a negative contribution, but they will be contributions nonetheless.

The question for the ethnographer, therefore, is to what extent are researchers able to contextualise these routines as they have been experienced by the participants in the communities being studied? If the aim of ethnography is to view social life *holistically*, rather than decontextualizing it and slicing it up according to some arbitrary scheme of evaluation, then the aim of the ethnographic researcher is to find a way to get as close as possible to the people in the community, then describe and explain how different "cultural domains constitute and influence each other" (Boellstorff et al., 2012, p. 3). Participant observation, therefore, allows the ethnographic researcher to situate their data within the context of experience, and to link those contexts through a plausible analysis when the time comes. In this way participant observation continues to offer a "flexible approach into the data analysis phase" (Boellstorff et al., 2012, p. 160).

16.1   Closing the Gap

A powerful advantage of the ethnographic method, then, is the way in which, through participant observation, the researcher is taken off their formal pedestal and is able to get close to the people they are observing. The common cultural conception (stereotype) that research is done by people with clipboards is a classic misnomer that is still often found in day-to-day life. Which means that, not only is there something of a methodological divide between the different traditions of social research, but there is also a divide between those who are being observed and those doing the observing. The aim of participant observation is to close that gap and for the researcher to experience the social routines, phenomenon and lifeworlds of the host communities, in a way that makes them coherent. The description of the task is simple, though often obscured in a competing field of investigative techniques. The practice of participant observation is defined as much by what is *observed* as by what is *participated* in. If there is no participative reflection and the researcher only stands back, takes notes, and does not get involved in the life of the community they are privileged to encounter, then they cannot gain access or empathy with the world as it is experienced.

According to Boellstorff *et al*, "ethnography is as much about doing – participating in everyday activities – as talking." (Boellstorff et al., 2012, p. 17). Being a participant observer, therefore, is a dual role in which the knowledge of the participants is valued because it is grounded *in situ*, and because it has been shared by the active members of the community that is being observed. Boellstorff *et al* identify three levels of engagement between the researcher and the participants in a study:

> "'Informant' signifies that members of a culture inform ethnographers, sharing understandings about their lives through conversation and participatory activity. 'Participants' suggests active sharing of

knowledge between members of a culture and ethnographers participating within it. 'Collaborator' is a term occasionally used in ethnographic projects with an explicit applied or activist component, to signal a shared set of goals" (Boellstorff et al., 2012, p. 17).

In this sense the ethnographic researcher is able to make comparisons between what people do and what they talk about doing. By maintaining this level of intimacy, the researcher who is grounded in the mundane practices which help to shape the daily lifeworlds of the collaborators, thus reaches different levels of sustained engagement. As Boellstorff *et al* elaborate:

> "While ethnographers are concerned with what people are up to, we are also concerned with their emic understandings of what they are doing and its significance to them. An important aspect of data analysis therefore involves comparing the interactions observed in participant observation with participant's own understandings and interpretations of these activities" (Boellstorff et al., 2012, p. 170).

16.2   Claims of Commensurability

Always in mind, moreover, is the question of commensurability between what is claimed and what is enacted. The role of the ethnographic researcher is to "discover what is happening in the field – what people actually do as they live their lives, unmindful of the analyst's protocols" (Boellstorff et al., 2012, p. 42). So by actively engaging with and participating in the culture of the collaborators, and in eschewing the vestiges of positivist objectivity, the ethnographic researcher is able to adapt their research as they progress to suit the surroundings and the environments in which they are participating. By keeping such an open view on the subjects of the study, the ethnographic researcher seeks to discover as much as possible from the emergent interactions. All that limits these interactions are the practical constraints of the fieldsites, the descriptive and observational skills of the researchers, and the reflective engagement that the researcher brings to the process. This is an alliance between "engaging in everyday activities, on the one hand, and recording and analysing those activities, on the other" (Boellstorff et al., 2012, p. 69).

It is a set of practices that run in parallel, and demands a high-level of interplay between the cognitive, observational and descriptive capabilities of the researcher. There is no way that the researcher can know in advance what the field of study will give-up. Instead the researcher has to be in the field and be present to observe them. And while the process of engagement with field sites and the communities that are of interest to us require a certain degree of fortitude and self-assurance on the part of the investigator, there is nothing more powerful than showing concern, interest and empathy for the people who are active in a community. Being tactful, respectful and discrete are the hallmarks of good observational practice. In contrast, however, being gregarious, willing and prepared to go with the flow, might offer a better route into participation, and therefore a fuller picture of what is being lived.

16.3   Hermeneutics and Interpretation

This paper started by noting the difference between an epistemological view of knowledge communities (*universitas*), and a hermeneutical view (*societas*), and has subsequently attempted to explain the distinction between quantitative methods of data collection and the qualitative approach to ethnographic study. Robert Prus offers a reminder that:

> "Those adopting a positivist (or positivist/structuralist) orientation generally take the viewpoint that human behaviour is a product of the forces, factors, or structures (internal and external) that act on people to generate particular outcomes" (Prus, 1996, p. 4).

In the positivist frame there is little room, according to Prus, for "human agency in the production of action" (Prus, 1996, p. 8). However, in contrast to this standpoint the interpretative, or hermeneutic tradition of investigation, focuses on the behaviours and the accomplishments of people acting in communities. As Prus summarises:

> "The interpretivists envision human group life as actively constituted by people in interaction with others. Human behaviour is seen as denoting an interpretative, interactive process. The primary methodological procedures are ethnographic (participant-observation, observation, and open-ended interviews) in nature. Human life is studied as it is experienced and accomplished by the very people involved in its production. The interpretivists are centrally concerned with the meanings people attach to their situations and the ways in which they go about constructing their activities in conjunction with others" (Prus, 1996, p. 9).

The interpretivists contend, therefore, that people are different from other objects and that the study of human behaviour, consequently, requires a methodology that is attentive to those differences. This requires a form of study that is rooted in "people's meanings, interpretations, activities, and interactions," and which will prefigure the lived experiences of those agents acting in those communities. As Prus points out "These notions […] are the essential substance of a social science" (Prus, 1996, p. 9).

16.4   Social Change Permissions

So, in developing this study, it is intended that the information collected and analysed would contribute towards a more practical review of the role of social and collaborative media. By developing a pragmatic/constructivist methodology, based on hermeneutics (i.e. interpretation and understanding), as opposed to the more positivistic and epistemic formulations of critical social theory, based as they are on the search for "hardcore reality" (Bernstein, 2010 p.123), this approach makes its contribution to knowledge in a way that highlights the *commensurable* and the *incommensurable* characteristics of the language used by participants in social media communities. And rather than looking for theoretical permission to bring about social change, based on abstract, positivist/realist theorising, or by inventing a set of metanarratives that seek to bind the seemingly incommensurable together (in an attractive political programme of emancipation for instance), the pragmatic approach instead seeks to define social and collaborative media as an example of, and an agent for, social change *in-itself*.

The task going forward, then is to map out how processes of creative understanding and meaning generation are practiced and experienced within different social groups, different social circumstances and at different times. As Robert Kozinets suggests:

42

"A good hermeneutic interpretation will delve into the social and historical contexts of the data for its explanations, providing a subtle, specific, nuanced cultural interpretation"(Kozinets, 2010, p. 120).

This approach views the study of culture, not as a system, structure or objective phenomenon, but instead, as what Richard Rorty calls a *conversation*. As Rorty explains:

"The notion of culture as a conversation rather than as a structure erected upon foundations fits well with the hermeneutical notion of knowledge, since getting into a conversation with strangers is like acquiring a new virtue or skill by imitating models" (Rorty, 2009, p. 319).

And it is the way that we enter into these conversations and the way that we understand them and structure them, either by skilful manipulation of language, or by imitating them to the point that they become purposeful, that is the objective of interpretative research, and thus the reason for drawing on the ethnographic tradition. As Rorty summarises:

"Such disciplinary matrices are studied by the usual empirical-cum-hermeneutic methods of 'cultural anthropology'. From the point of view of the group in question these subjective conditions are a combination of commonsensical practical imperatives (e.g. tribal taboos, Mill's methods) with the standard current theory about subjects" (Rorty, 2009, p. 385).

The aim here is not to 'prove' a theory or to 'fit' a model to the behaviour of certain social subjects, but instead to understand and offer a plausible explanation for the way that participants in these communities make sense of the *commensurability* of the *commonsensical imperatives* that shape their experiences. Therefore, the basis of this study is to relate to participants in communities of social and collaborative media networks as a *societas*.

16.5   Practice and Experience

According to Robert Kozinets, "as we understand various new social phenomena, we construct the meaning of methodological terms anew"(Kozinets, 2010, p. 62). As a study of social media, then, this approach aims to establish ethnographic research techniques that will allow investigators to observe and describe the language and accomplishments articulated by participants in communities who are engaged in collaborative media projects. It is therefore possible to ask about the extent to which the activities, attitudes and behaviours associated with social and collaborative media are represented in social studies models, and what the claims made about social media are that need to be validated against practice and experience? This entails looking at the relationships between different participants in this specific social network, and asking questions about the roles that different participants play?

Ultimately, this means identifying how participants make sense of their activities and function within their social environment; while at the same time, thinking about the way that the researcher impacted on the study merely by seeking to examine it? In doing this, it will be possible to demonstrate that qualitative ethnographic research is able to offer a purposeful viewpoint on the emerging social practices that are associated with social and collaborative media; while simultaneously commenting on a range of associated social issues that have significance in the wider context in which social and collaborative media is actively practiced. This wider context relates to the way that media production organisations and institutions operate, how audiences are organised and understood, and the way that individuals and social groups are able to make sense of their experience as active producers of media content in an on-going and dynamic conversation (as a community of practice). As David Silverman suggests, most ethnographic field researcher "thus attempt 'to get inside the black box' of social institutions to gain access to their interior processes and practices" (David Silverman in Miller & Dingwall, 1997 p.15). And it is the interior processes and practices of social and collaborative media that this ethnographic study attempts to describe.

To summarise:

- By using ethnographic research techniques our studies attempt to identify and validate the processes that are emerging through social and collaborative media participation.
- These processes are meaning driven, and depends on a specific and contingent social context to make sense.
- Information is collected and organised reflexively, with the experience of the researcher playing as important a role as the participants who are being represented.
- This information is drawn from experiences taking place in the field, through specific activities taking place in the main location of production and online.
- This information is represented using descriptive techniques.
- Theory and abstraction is only built-up once sufficient descriptive examples had been accumulated.

In addition, it is possible to uses the insights of a *constructivist* and *pragmatist* mode of ethnographic enquiry, the "symbolic interactionist perspective" as promoted by Herbert Blumer and Robert Prus (Blumer, 1953, 1966, 1969, 1990; Prus, 1997, p. 256), it is assumed that a holistic picture will be established of the participants and actors approaches to social and collaborative media interaction, which are best defined in their natural setting, "offering rich description and paying careful attention to the dynamics of the social process being examined" (Prus, 1997, p. 257). Using an aphorism coined by Prus, "the simple rule is that something significant is about to happen in the field," so it is the ethnographic researchers job to "be there" (Prus, 1997, p. 203).

In addition, and as Bourdieu suggests, "it is because subjects do not, strictly speaking, know what they are doing that what they are doing has more meaning than they know" (Bourdieu, 1977 p.79). It is not the function of this research approach, however, to assume that the researcher has any more sense of what is being done, and why, than the participants themselves. This is what will be left to be put together after a sufficiently compelling set of stories and narrative has been established. The question remains in this regard, though, how will we know that we are at the point where a sufficiently compelling story is ready to be told? It will be a significant aim of our studies, therefore, to identify the criteria against which this decision can usefully be made. One possible way to frame this question, however, is to think about the benefit that this narrative might have in helping others as they seek to make improvements to their working practices, or understand better the conversations that they are part of. As Martyn Denscome suggests:

44

> "The aim is 'to arrive at recommendations for good practice that will tackle a problem or enhance the performance of the organisation and individuals through changes to the rules and procedures within which they operate' (Denscombe 2002: 27 quoted in Bell, 2005, p. 8).

This is a far cry from a universalistic or positivist intervention in social functions, but it is no less laudable to aim for such a practical outcome.

17   Primary Frameworks

It is worth noting some final comments that reveal the ongoing challenge of this way of thinking from a conceptual point of view. This process of structuration of roles and role-taking, which is accordingly expressed through different 'frameworks,' give substance to the differing conceptual schemes that recur within a culture. Organising the rules and the definitions that accompany concepts into primary and subsidiary frameworks might, as Anthony Giddens suggests, indicate that "whatever its level of organisation, a primary framework allows individuals to categorise an indefinite plurality of circumstances or situations so as to be able to respond in an appropriate fashion to whatever is going on" (Giddens, 1984, p. 88). Individuals, therefore, who make sense of, sustain and promote a 'primary framework' of meaning are positioned as 'actors' who understand the "rules of language [and] of primary and secondary framing." These agents are thus able, at the same time, to conduct themselves over "large areas of social life" (Giddens, 1984, p. 89) in both adaptive and imaginative ways.

The point here, according to Giddens, is that while frameworks of reference exist for individuals within communities, they are neither *determined* nor *programmed* by those frameworks, but instead act with a *recursive degree of agency*, interdependence and independence, against a background of claim and counter-claim. Therefore, it is important to follow Richard Rorty's instruction to seek to identify the *congruent* from the *incongruent* language that we use, because we will always grow out of and tire of the existing frames of reference that we presently take for granted. Moreover, and rather than having these definitions imposed and defined for us, we should consider the extent to which it be possible for agents and actors in the social realm to shape and define, what Rorty calls, a *common vocabulary* for themselves. As Rorty points out,

> What binds societies together are common vocabularies and common hopes. The vocabularies are typically parasitic on the hopes – in the sense that the principle function of the vocabularies is to tell stories about future outcomes which compensate for present sacrifices (Rorty, 1989 p.86).

We might subsequently ask ourselves the question, as Michael Oakeshott suggests, do we want to do this on the basis that we are a society predominantly organised as a *universitas* or as a *societas*? What is a more relevant question than how do we make sense of, and give due importance to, the every-day practices and experiences of the participants who volunteer in social media groups? We might be better explaining participation, on the one hand, as a form of social knowledge that is exchanged within a *'societas,'* that is a group of people who share their corresponding life experiences together; or alternatively, as a set of social arrangements that takes the form of a *'universitas'*, in which there is a mutual self-interest between a group of people who want to achieve a particular goal or outcome (Oakeshott, 1975). Either way, the challenge is to find out what people do from first-hand accounts, as Blumer suggests, as they take place as a form of meaningful accomplishment.

18 References

Amit, V. (2000). *Constructug the Field: Ethnographic Fieldwork in the Contemporary World*. London: Routledge.

Bauman, Z., & May, T. (2001). *Thinking Sociologically* (2nd ed.). Oxford: Blackwell.

Bell, J. (2005). *Doing Your Research Project* (4th ed.). Oxford: Oxford University Press.

Bernstein, R. J. (2010). *The Pragmatic Turn*. London: Polity.

Blumer, H. (1953). Psychological Import of the Human Group. In M. Sherif & M. O. Wilson (Eds.), Group Relations at the Crossroads. New York: Harper & Row.

Blumer, H. (1966). Sociological Implications of the Thought of George Herbert Mead. *American Journal of Sociology, 71*, 535-548.

Blumer, H. (1969). *Symbolic Interactionism*. Berkley, CA: University of California Press.

Blumer, H. (1990). *Industrialisation as an Agent of Social Change - A Critical Analysis* (D. R. Maines & T. J. Morrione Eds.). New York: Aldine de Gruyter.

Blumer, H., & Shibutani, T. (1973). *Human Nature and Collective Behavior: Papers in Honor of Herbert Blumer*. New Brunswick: Transaction Books.

Boellstorff, T., Nardi, B., Pearce, C., & Taylor, T. L. (2012). *Ethnography and Virtual Worlds*. Princeton: Princeton University Press.

Bourdieu, P. (1977). *Outline of a Theory of Practice* (R. Nice, Trans.). Cambridge: Cambridge University Press.

Crang, M., & Cook, I. (2007). *Doing Ethnographies*. London: Sage.

Creswell, J. W. (1994). *Research Design: Qualitative and Quantative Approaches*. London: Sage.

Creswell, J. W. (1998). *Qualitative Inquiry and Research Design - Choosing Among Five Traditions*. London: Sage.

Davis, C. A. (1999). *Reflexive Ethnography*. London: Routledge.

Dewey, J. (1910). *How We Think*. New York: D.C. Heath.

Flick, U. (2009). *An Introduction to Qualitative Research Design*. London: Sage.

Giddens, A. (1984). *The Constitution of Society*. Oxford: Polity Press.

Glaser, B. G. (1998). *Doing Grounded Theory - Issues and Discussions*. Mill Valley, CA: Sociology Press.

Goffman, E. (1990). *The Presentation of the Self in Everyday Life*. London: Punguin.

Guimaraes, M. J. L. (2005). Doing Anthropology in Cyberspace: Fieldwork Boundaries and Social Environments. In C. Hine (Ed.), *Virtual Methods: Issues in Social Research on the Internet* (pp. 141-156). Oxford: Berg.

Hine, C. (Ed.) (2005). *Virtual Methods - Issues in social Research on the Internet*. Oxford: Berg.

Jenkins, H. (2006). *Convergence Culture - Where Old and New Media Collide*. New York: New York University Press.

Kozinets, R. V. (2010). *Netnography - Doing Ethnographic Research Online*. London: Sage.

McCarthy, J., & Wright, P. (2004). *Technology as Experience*. Cambridge, Massachusetts: The MIT Press.

Miller, G., & Dingwall, R. (Eds.). (1997). *Context & Method in Qualitative Research*. London: Sage.

Mills, C. W. (1959). *The Sociological Imagination*. Oxford: Oxford University Press.

Oakeshott, M. (1975). *On Human Conduct*. Oxford: Oxford University Press.

Prus, R. (1996). *Symbolic Interactionism and Ethnographic Research*. New York: State University of New York Press.

Prus, R. (1997). *Subcultural Mosaics and Intersubjective Realities*. New York: State University of New York Press.

Prus, R. (1999). *Beyond the Power Mystique*. New York: State University of New York Press.

Rorty, R. (1989). *Contingency, Irony, and Solidarity*. Cambridge: Cambridge University Press.

Rorty, R. (2009). *Philosophy and the Mirror of Nature* (30th Aniversary Edition ed.). Princeton: Princeton University Press.

Schensul, S. L., Schensul, J. J., & LeCompte, M. D. (1999). *Essential Ethnographic Methods: Observations, Interviews, and Questionnaires*. Walnut Creek, CA: Altamira Press.

Schneider, S. M., & Foot, K. A. (2005). Web Sphere Analysis: An Approach to Studying Online Action. In C. Hine (Ed.), *Virtual Methods: Issues in Social Research on the Internet* (pp. 157-170). Oxford: Berg.

Shickman, A. (1978). The "Perspective Glass" in Shakespeare's Richard II. *Studies in English Literature, 1500-1900, 18*(2), 217-228.

Struwig, F. W., & Stread, G. (2001). *Planning, Designing and Reporting Research*. Cape Town: Maskew Miller Longman.

Tapscott, D. (2008). *Grown Up Digital - How the Net Generation is Changing Your World*. London: McGraw-Hill Professional.

Wenger, E. (1998). *Communities of Practice*. Cambridge: Cambridge University Press.